D1097569

Simple **Crocheted Hats**

Simple Crocheted Hats

15 BEAUTIFUL DESIGNS TO CREATE WITH EASE

VANESSA MOONCIE

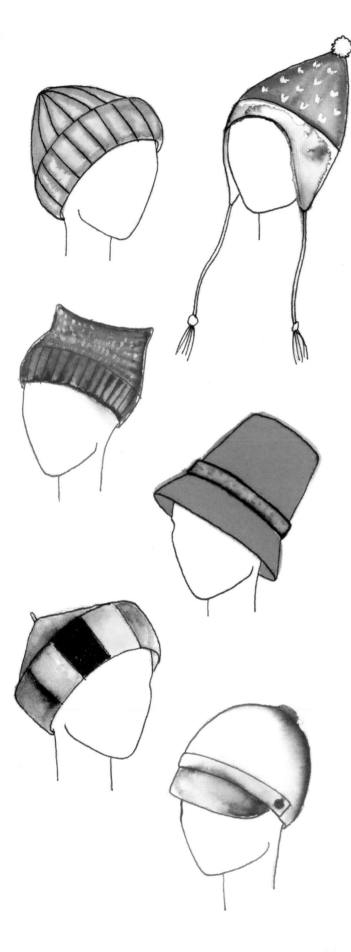

Contents

Introduction

I love hats; I have quite a collection of them. So I was very happy to be asked to design a range of simple hats to crochet for this book. I endeavoured to create a collection in a variety of styles that were suitable for wearing in all seasons.

There are fifteen projects here, including a number of hats to keep you warm and cosy, such as the Hooded Scarf (page 90) and the Colourblock Beanie (page 94). The Pinwheel Beret (page 104) and Bowler Hat (page 114) are designed to be worn in any season or for an informal event.

The choice of yarn can transform a project. The Wide-brimmed Hat (page 44), for example, can be crocheted in wool to wear on a chilly day or, following the same pattern, made in raffia yarn for a sun hat.

Instructions for each hat are given in three sizes, to fit a head circumference of up to 20, 22 and 24in (51, 56 and 61cm). At the back of the book there is a techniques section that will give you all the information you need on getting started, illustrated step-by-step instructions on the crochet stitches used in the patterns, joining in colours and sewing the seams.

The hats are worked in rounds or rows of crochet, using various basic stitches to produce different effects. Crocheting into a single loop of each stitch forms the rib on the Square Hat (page 36), and a simple colour change creates the pattern on the Nordic-style Fairisle Hat with Earflaps (page 78).

All of the projects have charts to accompany the written instructions to make it easy to follow the patterns. Most of the hats can be finished within a day and would make a quick and versatile addition to your wardrobe.

THE PROJECTS

Peaked Cap

The peak is stiffened with buckram, and the cap is finished with decorative crocheted buttons stitched on a strap and at the top of the hat.

MATERIALS
Rico Essentials Alpaca Blend Chunky, 50% acrylic, 30% virgin wool, 20% alpaca (98yd/90m per 50g ball), or any chunky yarn: 2[2:2] x 50g balls in 003 Pebble (A)

5mm (UK6:USH/8) and 5.5mm (UK5:USI/9) crochet hooks

9 x 3in (23 x 7.5cm) heavyweight buckram

Scissors

Pencil

Blunt-ended yarn needle

SIZE
To fit: up to 20[22:24]in (51[56:61]cm) head circumference

TENSION
14 sts and 14 rows to 4in (10cm) over double crochet on 5.5mm hook. Use larger or smaller hook if necessary to obtain correct tension.

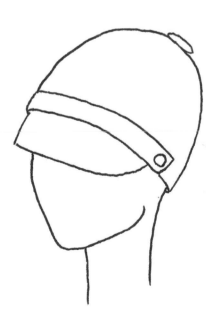

METHOD

The crown is worked in continuous rounds of double crochet. The peak and peak facing are crocheted in rows. The buckram is cut to size, using the crocheted peak as a template. The buckram is sandwiched between the peak and the facing, and an edging of double crochet is worked around the back of the cap and into both peak pieces at the same time to enclose the buckram. A strap is attached to the front of the hat with two small crocheted buttons that are stitched through all layers. A larger crocheted button is sewn to the top of the cap.

CROWN

Starting at the top of the crown, with 5.5mm hook and A, make a magic loop (see page 132).

Round 1: 1 ch, 6 dc into loop (6 sts).

Round 2 (inc): (Dc2inc) 6 times (12 sts). Pull tightly on short end of yarn to close loop.

Round 3 (inc): (Dc2inc, 1 dc) 6 times (18 sts).

Round 4 (inc): (Dc2inc, 2 dc) 6 times (24 sts).

Round 5 (inc): (Dc2inc, 3 dc) 6 times (30 sts).

Continue increasing 6 sts on each round as set until there are 66[72:78] sts.

Next: 1 dc in each dc without shaping until work measures 6¼[7:7¾]in (16[18:19.5]cm) from top of hat.

KEY

$\mathcal{O}$	chain (ch)
•	slip stitch (sl st)
✛	double crochet (dc)
✕✕	dc2inc
✕✕	dc2tog
✛∪	dc in front loop only
✛∩	dc in back loop only

CROWN
Size 20in (51cm)
Rounds 1 to end

Sizes 22–24in (56–61cm)
Rounds 1–11

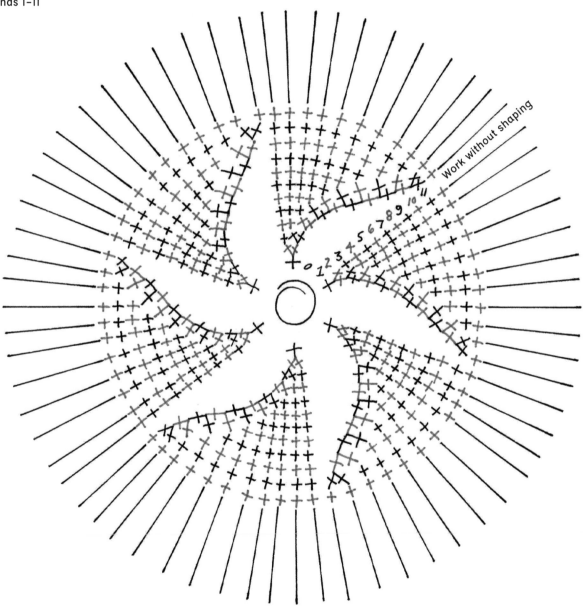

Work without shaping

0 1 2 3 4 5 6 7 8 9 10 11

CROWN
Size 22in (56cm)
Rounds 12 to end

Size 24in (61cm)
Round 12

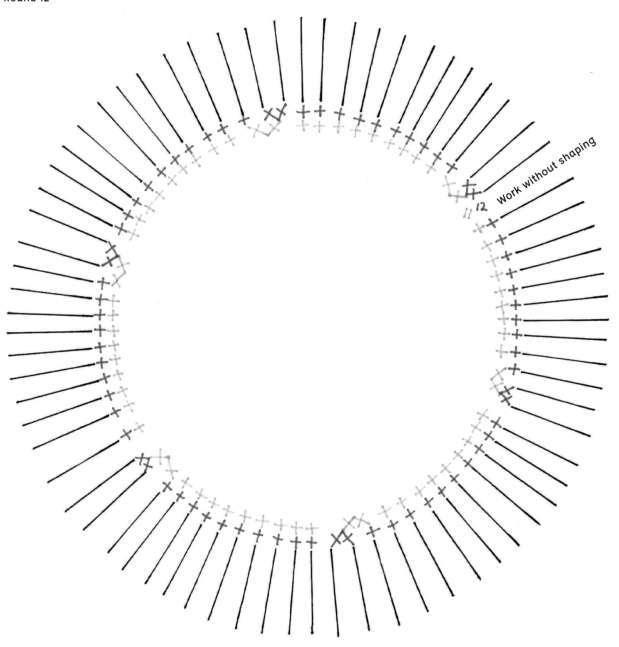

Work without shaping

11 12

CROWN
Size 24in (61cm)
Rounds 13 to end

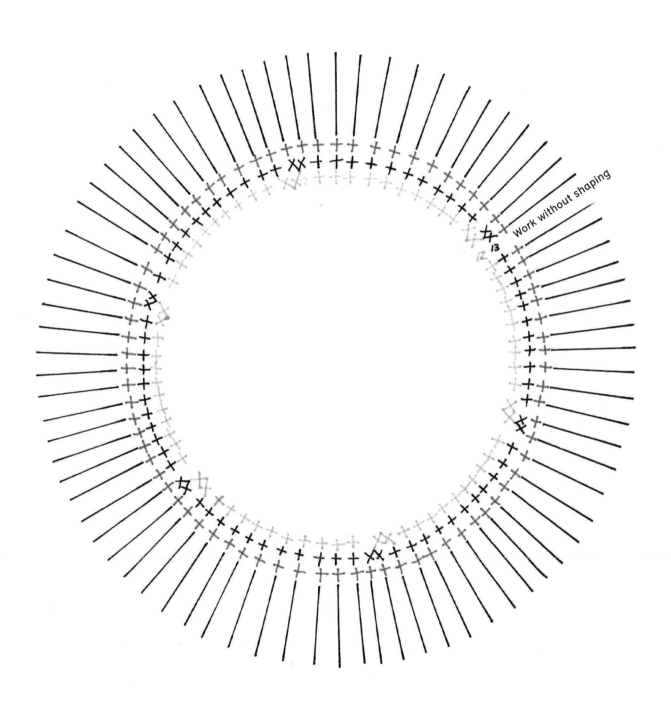

Work without shaping

13

PEAK

Row 1: 1 dc in front loop only of next 28[30:32] dc, turn.

Continue in both loops of these 28[30:32] sts.

Row 2: 1 ch, skip first dc, 1 dc in next 26[28:30] dc, sl st in next dc, turn.

Row 3: 1 ch, skip first dc, 1 dc in next 24[26:28] dc, sl st in next dc, turn.

Row 4: 1 ch, skip first dc, 1 dc in next 22[24:26] dc, sl st in next dc, turn.

Row 5: 1 ch, skip first dc, 1 dc in next 20[22:24] dc, sl st in next dc, turn.

Row 6: 1 ch, skip first dc, 1 dc in next 18[20:22] dc, sl st in next dc, turn.

Row 7: 1 ch, skip first dc, 1 dc in next 16[18:20] dc, sl st in next dc, turn.

Row 8: 1 ch, skip first dc, 1 dc in next 14[16:18] dc, sl st in next dc, turn.

Sizes 22–24in (56–61cm) only

Row 9: 1 ch, skip first dc, 1 dc in next [14:16] dc, sl st in next dc, turn.

Size 24in (61cm) only

Row 10: 1 ch, skip first dc, 1 dc in next 14 dc, sl st in next dc.

All sizes

Fasten off.

PEAK FACING

With RS of cap facing, rejoin A with a sl st to the back loop of the first 28[30:32] dc at the base of the peak.

Row 1: 1 dc in same st as sl st, 1 dc in back loop only of next 27[29:31] dc, turn.

Rows 2–8[9:10]: Work as for rows 2–8[9:10] of peak. Fasten off.

Lay the crocheted peak flat on the buckram and draw around it with a pencil. Cut around the pencil line with scissors.

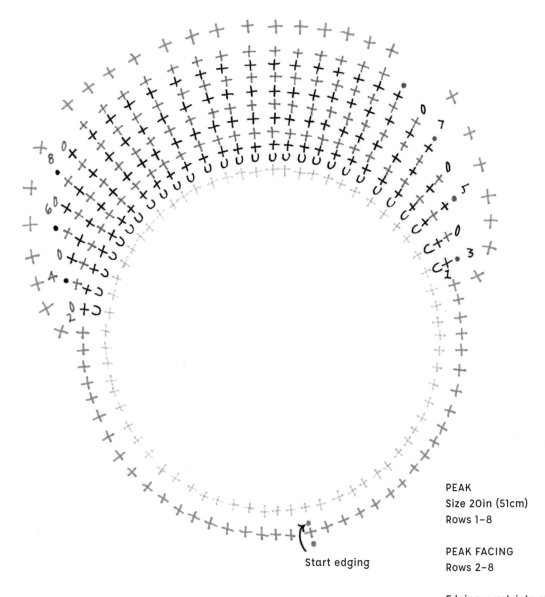

Start edging

PEAK
Size 20in (51cm)
Rows 1–8

PEAK FACING
Rows 2–8

Edging: work into stitches of peak and peak facing at same time to join

PEAK
Size 22in (56cm)
Rows 1–9

PEAK FACING
Rows 2–9

Edging: work into stitches of
peak and peak facing at same
time to join

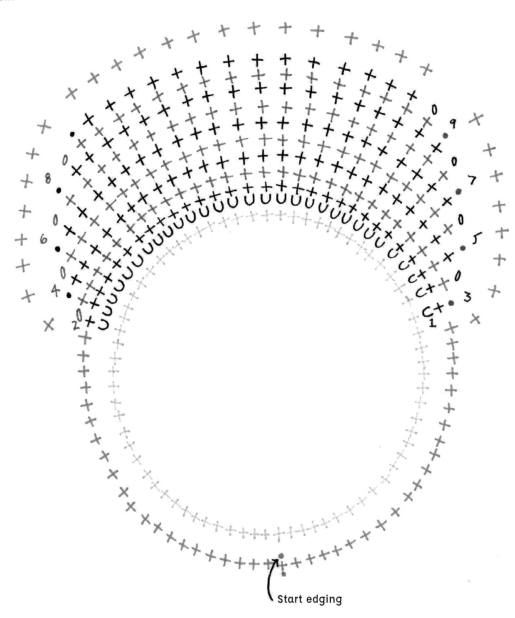

Start edging

PEAK
Size 24in (61cm)
Rows 1–10

PEAK FACING
Rows 2–10

Edging: work into stitches of
peak and peak facing at same
time to join

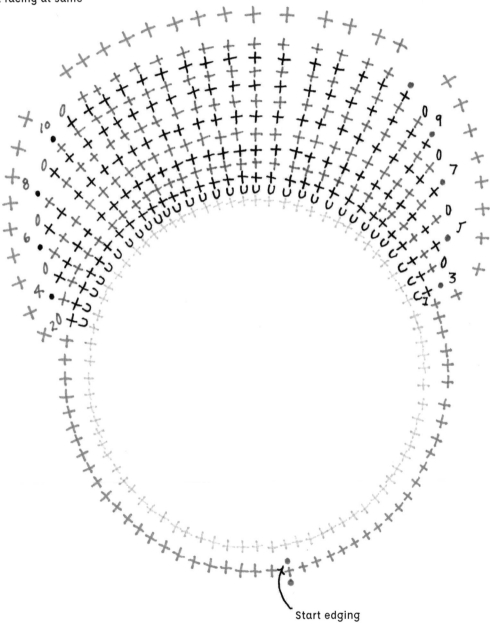

Start edging

EDGING

With RS facing, skip the first 19[21:23] dc and rejoin A with a sl st in the next dc at the back of the cap.
Next: 1 dc in same dc as sl st, 1 dc in next 18[20:22] dc, place buckram between the peak and peak facing; working in both peak and peak facing at same time to join and encase the buckram, work 7[8:9] dc evenly down first side of peak, 1 dc into next 14 dc at front of peak pieces, work 7[8:9] dc evenly up other side of peak, 1 dc in next 19[21:23] dc. Sl st in next st and fasten off.

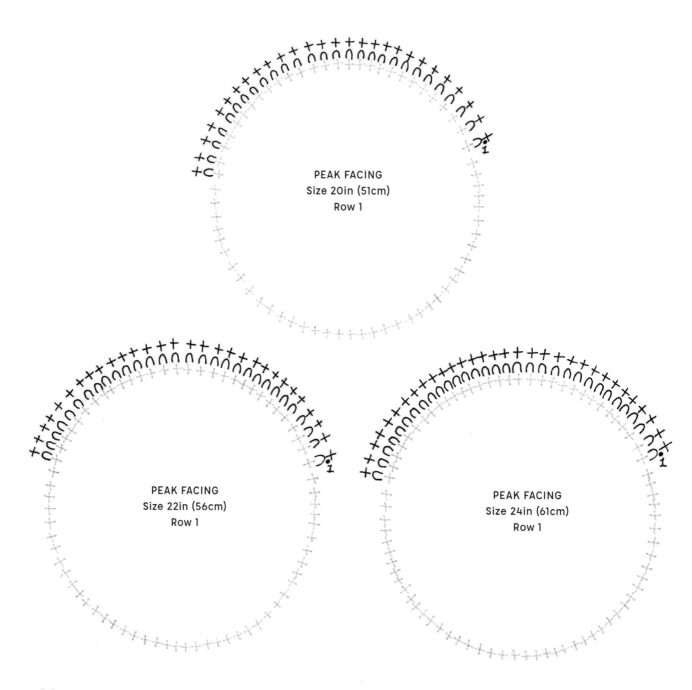

PEAK FACING
Size 20in (51cm)
Row 1

PEAK FACING
Size 22in (56cm)
Row 1

PEAK FACING
Size 24in (61cm)
Row 1

STRAP

With 5.5mm hook and A, make 41[43:45] ch.

Round 1: 1 dc in second ch from hook, 1 dc in next 38[40:42] ch, 2 dc in end ch, 1 dc in reverse side of next 39[41:43] ch (80[84:88] sts). Sl st in next st and fasten off.

STRAP
Round 1

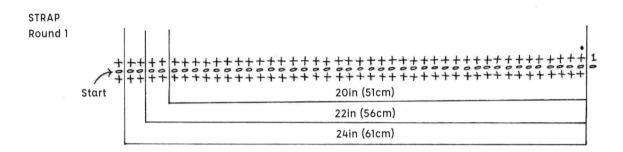

Start

20in (51cm)

22in (56cm)

24in (61cm)

LARGE BUTTON

With 5.5mm hook and A, make a magic loop.

Rounds 1–2 (inc): Work as for rounds 1–2 of crown (12 sts).

Rounds 3–5: 1 dc in each dc.

Round 6 (dec): (Dc2tog) 6 times (6 sts). Fasten off, leaving a long tail of yarn at the end.

LARGE BUTTON
Rounds 1–6

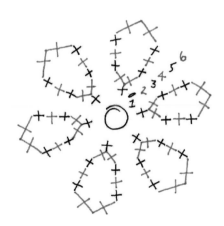

SMALL BUTTON (MAKE 2)

With 5mm hook and A, make a magic loop.

Round 1: 1 ch, 5 dc into loop (5 sts).

Round 2 (inc): (Dc2inc) 5 times (10 sts). Pull tightly on short end of yarn to close loop.

Round 3 (dec): (Dc2tog) 5 times (5 sts). Fasten off, leaving a long tail of yarn at the end.

SMALL BUTTON
Rounds 1–3

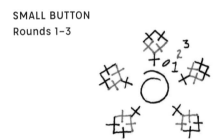

MAKING UP

Thread tails of yarn through last round of the buttons. Flatten the buttons and sew a few stitches through the centre of each one. Stitch the large button to the top of the cap. Place the strap across the centre front of the cap and sew a small button to each end of the strap, stitching through to the cap to secure it in place. Weave in yarn ends.

Plaid Hat

Stripes of double crochet and treble stitches form the background of this plaid design. Vertical lines of slip stitch finish the hat, topped with a tufty adornment of loops and knotted lengths of chain stitches.

MATERIALS
Drops Cotton Light, 50% cotton, 50% polyester (115yd/105m per 50g ball), or any DK yarn:
1[2:2] x 50g balls in 14 Turquoise (A)
1[1:2] x 50g balls in 27 Mint (B)

3.25mm (UK10:USD/3) and 3.5mm (UK9:USE/4) crochet hooks

Blunt-ended yarn needle

SIZE
To fit: up to 20[22:24]in (51[56:61]cm) head circumference

TENSION
17 sts and 10 rows to 4in (10cm) over pattern on 3.5mm hook. Use larger or smaller hook if necessary to obtain correct tension.

METHOD

The rib is worked from side to side, crocheting into the back loop of each stitch. The crown of the hat is crocheted in rows of treble stitches with chain stitches made at equal intervals. The wide, horizontal bands are broken with narrow stripes of double crochet in a contrasting colour. The vertical lines are formed by working slip stitches through the chain spaces up the hat. Loops and lengths of chain stitch create a tasselled pompom when the top of the hat is gathered up.

RIB

Starting at the side of the ribbing, with 3.25mm hook and A, make 8 ch.

Row 1: 1 dc in second ch from hook, 1 dc in next 6 ch, turn (7 sts).

Rows 2–85[95:105]: 1 ch (does not count as a st throughout), 1 dc in back loop only of each dc, turn.

CROWN

Change to 3.5mm hook.

Row 1 (RS): 1 ch (does not count as a st throughout), work 85[95:105] dc evenly down the edge of the ribbing, turn (85[95:105] sts).

Row 2 (WS) (inc): 1 ch, 1 dc in next 0[5:0] dc, (dc2inc, 5[5:6] dc) 14[15:15] times, (dc2inc) 1[0:0] time (100[110:120] sts), turn.

Join in yarn B. Carry unused yarn up the wrong side of the work at the beginning of each round.

KEY

⌒	chain (ch)
•	slip stitch (sl st)
+	double crochet (dc)
⊤	double crochet in back loop only
⊤	treble (tr)
✕✕	dc2inc
✕✕	dc2dec

RIB
All sizes

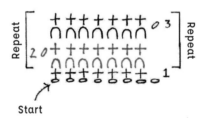

Start

CROWN
Size 22in (56cm)
Rows 1–2

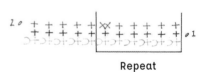

Repeat

CROWN
Size 20in (51cm)
Rows 1–2

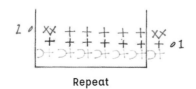

Repeat

CROWN
Size 24in (61cm)
Rows 1–2

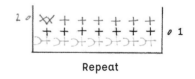

Repeat

Row 3: With B, sl st in first dc, 3 ch (counts as first tr throughout), 1 tr in next dc, 1 ch, (skip next dc, 1 tr in next 4 dc, 1 ch) 19[21:23] times, skip next dc, 1 tr in next 2 dc, sl st in third of 3 ch at beg of row to join, turn.

Row 4: 3 ch, 1 tr in next 2 tr, 1 ch, (skip next ch, 1 tr in next 4 tr, 1 ch) 19[21:23] times, skip next ch, 1 tr in next tr, sl st in third of 3 ch, turn.

Row 5: With A, 1 ch (does not count as a st), 1 dc in same st as sl st, 1 dc in each tr and ch sp, sl st in first dc, turn.

CROWN
Size 20in (51cm)
Rows 3–5

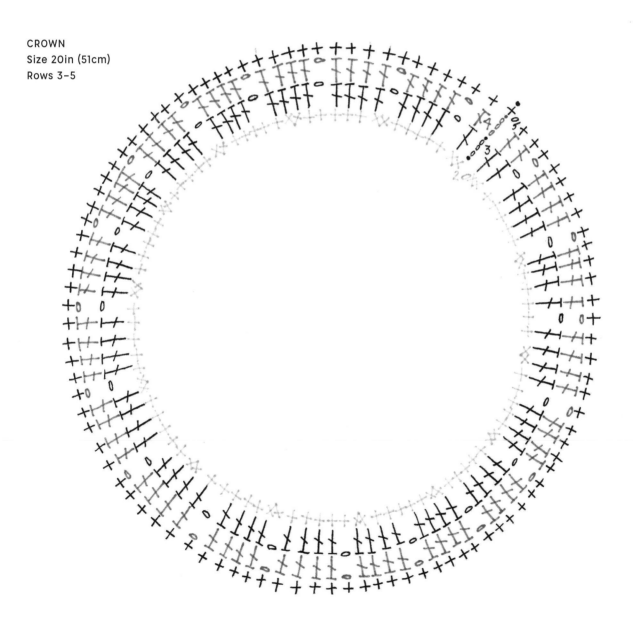

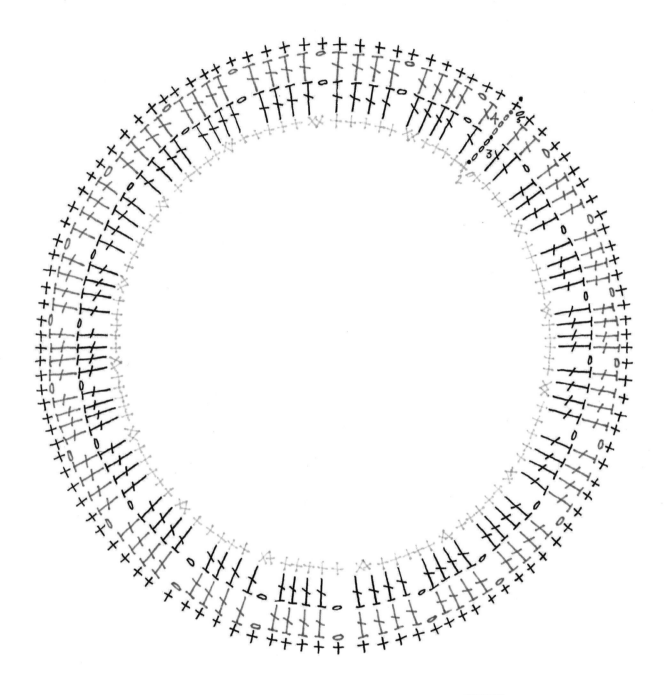

CROWN
Size 22in (56cm)
Rows 3–5

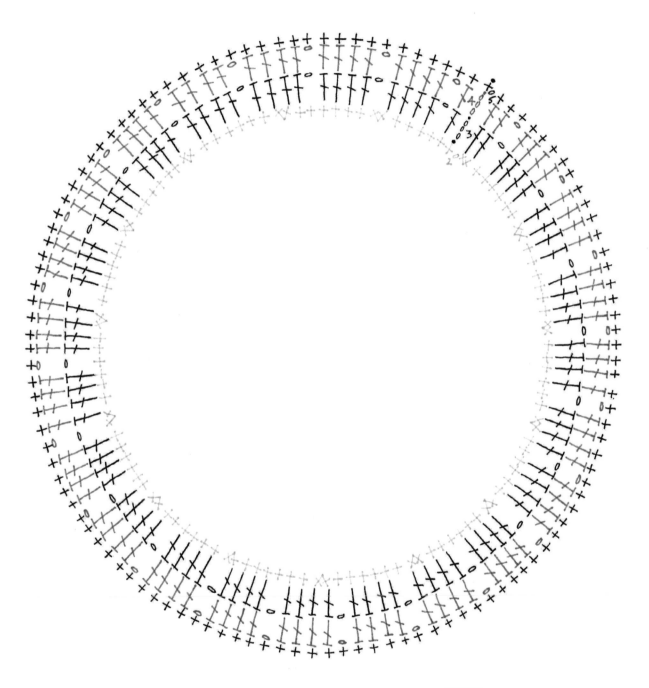

CROWN
Size 24in (61cm)
Rows 3–5

Row 6: With B, 3 ch, 1 tr in next 2 dc, 1 ch, (skip next dc, 1 tr in next 4 dc, 1 ch) 19[21:23] times, skip next dc, 1 tr in next dc, sl st in third of 3 ch, turn.

Row 7: 3 ch, 1 tr in next tr, 1 ch, (skip next ch, 1 tr in next 4 tr, 1 ch) 19[21:23] times, skip next ch, 1 tr in next 2 tr, sl st in third of 3 ch, turn.

Rows 8–9: With A, rep rows 6–7.

Row 10: With B, rep row 5.

Row 11: With A, 3 ch, 1 tr in next dc, 1 ch, (skip next dc, 1 tr in next 4 dc, 1 ch) 19[21:23] times, skip next dc, 1 tr in next 2 dc, sl st in third of 3 ch, turn.

Row 12: With A, 3 ch, 1 tr in next 2 tr, 1 ch, (skip next ch, 1 tr in next 4 tr, 1 ch) 19[21:23] times, skip next ch, 1 tr in next tr, sl st in third of 3 ch, turn.

Row 13: With B, rep row 7.

Row 14: Rep row 6.

Row 15: Rep row 5.

Rows 16–17: With B, rep rows 6–7.

CROWN
All sizes
Rows 6–17

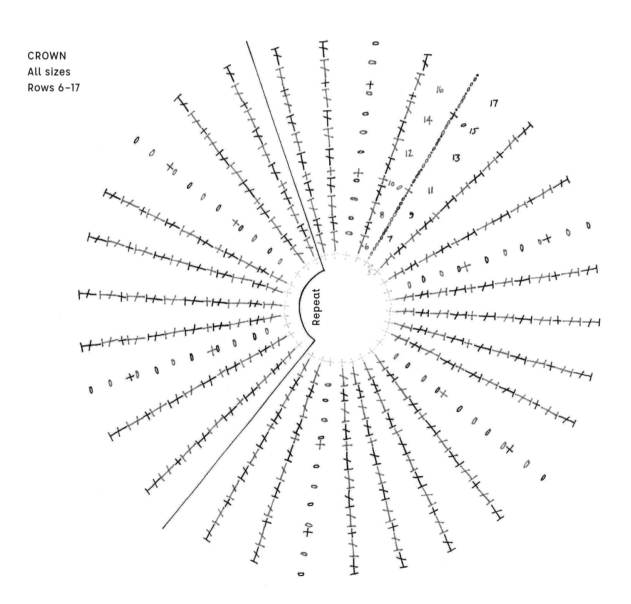

Sizes 22–24in (56–61cm) only

Rows 18–19: With A, rep rows 6-7. Follow rows 6-7 of chart on page 30.

Size 24in (61cm) only

Row 20: With B, rep row 5.
Row 21: With A, rep row 11.
Follow row 5 from chart on page 29 and row 11 from chart on page 30.

All sizes

Row 18[20:22]: With B[A:A], 1 ch, 1 dc in same st as sl st, 1 dc in each tr, skip each ch sp, sl st in first dc, turn (80[88:96] sts).
Row 19[21:23]: 1 ch, starting in same st as sl st, dc2tog to end (40[44:48] sts). Sl st in first st and fasten off, leaving a long tail of yarn B[A:A] at the end.

CROWN
All sizes
Rows 18[20:22]–19[21:23]

MAKING UP

Sew together the short edges of the rib. With right side of hat facing, 3.5mm hook and A, join yarn with a sl st to an unworked stitch on row 2 of the crown. Sl st up the vertical 1 ch sps, extending the loop of each stitch to the level of the top of the next ch sp being worked so they are not too tight; sl st in the st of the last row above the line of ch sps, make 20[30:30] ch, sl st in same st as last sl st to form a loop, make 10[15:15] ch, fasten off. Repeat with B on the next vertical set of chain spaces. Continue as before, alternating the yarns to complete the lines of surface crochet on the hat. Thread the long tail of yarn, left after fastening off the hat, through the last row of stitches. Keep the loops and lengths of chains on the right side of the hat and take care not to catch them in the stitches. Pull tightly on the tail of yarn to gather the top of the hat and fasten off securely. Trim the ends of the chain lengths to neaten. Weave in all ends.

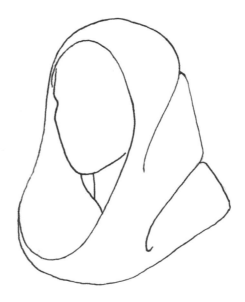

Cowl Hood

Double crochet and treble stitches form the pattern of this versatile accessory, which can be worn as a cosy hood or a cowl.

MATERIALS
Drops Eskimo, 100% wool (54yd/50m per 50g ball), or any super chunky yarn: 5[9:10] x 50g balls in 47 Light Beige Mix (A)

10mm (UK 000:USN-P/15) crochet hook

Blunt-ended yarn needle

SIZE
To fit: up to 20[22:24]in (51[56:61]cm) head circumference

TENSION
8 sts and 7 rows to 4in (10cm) over pattern on 10mm hook. Use larger or smaller hook if necessary to obtain correct tension.

METHOD

The hood is worked in rows of alternating double crochet and treble stitches to create the textured pattern. The short ends are stitched together to form a tube of fabric.

NOTE

If substituting for another yarn, be aware that some super chunky yarns are more dense than the one used for this project, so will create a much firmer fabric. Compare hook size and tension information on the ball bands to find a suitable substitute.

MAIN PIECE

With 10mm hook and A, make 57[73:77] ch.

Row 1: 1 dc in second ch from hook, 1 tr in next ch, (1 dc in next ch, 1 tr in next ch) to end, turn (56[72:76] sts).

Row 2: 1 ch (does not count as a st throughout), (1 dc in next tr, 1 tr in next dc) to end, turn. Rep row 2 until work measures 16[20:22]in (40.5[51:56]cm). Fasten off, leaving a long tail of yarn at the end.

MAKING UP

Use the tail of yarn to sew together the short edges, matching the rows. Weave in all ends.

RIB
All sizes

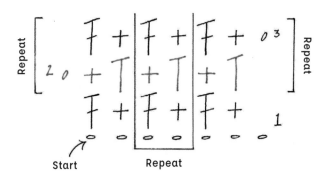

KEY

$\mathcal{O}$ chain (ch)

$+$ double crochet (dc)

$\overline{\mathsf{F}}$ treble (tr)

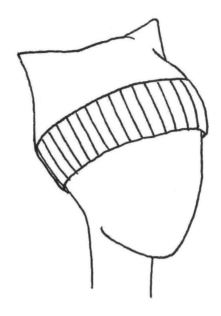

Square Hat

The square hat is worked entirely in rows of double crochet with no shaping at all. When the hat is worn, the corners at the top of the hat form little ears.

MATERIALS
King Cole Chunky Tweed, 72% premium acrylic, 25% wool, 3% viscose (151yd/138m per 100g ball), or any chunky yarn: 1[1:2] x 100g balls in 1082 Lewis (A)

6mm (UK4:USJ/10) crochet hook

Blunt-ended yarn needle

SIZE
To fit: up to 20[22:24]in (51[56:61]cm) head circumference

TENSION
12 sts and 14 rows to 4in (10cm) over double crochet on 6mm hook. Use larger or smaller hook if necessary to obtain correct tension.

METHOD

The rib is worked from side to side, crocheting into the back loop of each stitch to create the ribbed effect. The first row of the crown of the hat is crocheted into each stitch down one side of the rib. The hat is continued in rows of double crochet. The short edges are sewn together, and the stitches at the top of the hat are joined to form a straight seam to finish the hat.

RIB

Starting at the side of the ribbing, with 6mm hook and A, make 7[8:9] ch.
Row 1: 1 dc in second ch from hook, 1 dc in next 5[6:7] ch, turn (6[7:8] sts).
Rows 2–54[60:66]: 1 ch (does not count as a st throughout), 1 dc in back loop only of each dc, turn.

CROWN

Row 1: 1 ch, work 54[60:66] dc evenly down the edge of the ribbing, turn (54[60:66] sts).
Row 2: 1 ch, 1 dc in each dc, turn.
Rep row 2 until work measures 7¹/₂[8¹/₄:8⁷/₈]in (19[21:22.5]cm) from the beginning. Fasten off, leaving a long tail of yarn at the end.

MAKING UP

Use the long tail of yarn left after fastening off to sew together the short edges, matching the rows. Flatten the hat and sew the stitches of the last row on each side together to form a straight seam at the top. Weave in all ends.

KEY

𝒐 chain (ch)

⋔ double crochet in back loop only

╋ double crochet (dc)

RIB
All sizes
Rows 1–54[60:66]

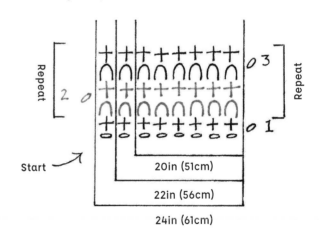

All sizes
CROWN
Rows 1 to end

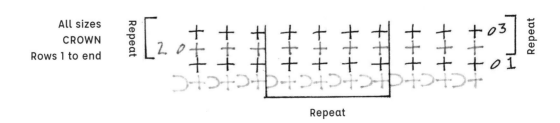

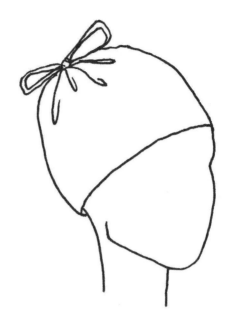

Tie-top Hat

This hat is worked in rows to create a straight strip of fabric. A crocheted drawstring gathers the top of the hat, forming the finished shaping.

MATERIALS
Rico Creative Cotton DK, 100% cotton (126yd/115m per 50g ball), or any DK yarn: 2[2:2] x 50g balls in 015 Teal (A)

4mm (UK8:USG/6) crochet hook

Blunt-ended yarn needle

SIZE
To fit: up to 20[22:24]in (51[56:61]cm) head circumference

TENSION
19 sts and 12 rows to 4in (10cm) over half treble on 4mm hook. Use larger or smaller hook if necessary to obtain correct tension.

METHOD

The hat is worked in rows throughout. Each eyelet is made by working two double crochet and two chain stitches, skipping the two stitches from the previous row to create a space in the fabric. In the next row, double crochet stitches are worked into each stitch and chain space. The main part of the hat is continued in half treble stitches and finished with an edging of double crochet stitches. The tie cord is made by working double crochet stitches into a length of chain stitches. The short edges of the hat are sewn together. The cord is threaded through the eyelets and tied in a tight bow to gather up the top of the hat.

NOTE

1 ch and 2 ch at beg of the row does not count as a st throughout.

MAIN PIECE

With 4mm hook and A, make 89[97:105] ch.
Row 1: 1 dc in 2nd ch from hook, 1 dc in each ch to end, turn (88[96:104] sts).
Row 2: 1 ch, (1 dc in next dc, 2 ch, skip 2 dc, 1 dc in next dc) 22[24:26] times, turn.
Row 3: 1 ch, (1 dc in next dc, 2 dc in next 2 ch sp, 1 dc in next dc) 22[24:26] times, turn.
Row 4: 2 ch, 1 htr in each st to end, turn.
Rep last row until work measures 6¾[7:7¾]in (17[18:19.5]cm) from beg.

EDGING

Rows 1–4: 1 ch, 1 dc in each dc, turn.
Fasten off, leaving a long tail of yarn at the end.

KEY

𝑜   chain (ch)

+   double crochet (dc)

⊤   half treble (htr)

HAT
All sizes

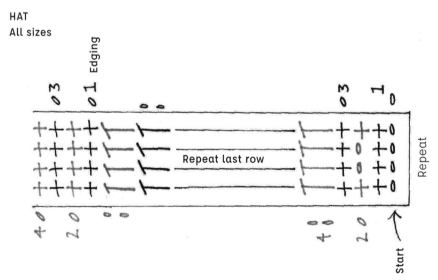

TIE CORD

With 4mm hook and A, make a 28[29½:31]in (71[75:79]cm) length of ch sts.

Next: 1 dc in 2nd ch from hook, 1 dc in each ch to end. Fasten off.

MAKING UP

Sew together the short edges. Thread the cord through the eyelets and tie in a bow to gather up the top of the hat. Weave in all ends.

TIE CORD
All sizes

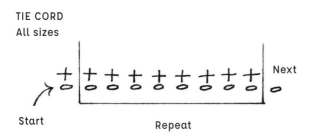

Wide-brimmed hat

Crocheted in super chunky yarn, this is a quick project to make. Use a wool-blend yarn for a chic accessory to wear on an autumnal day, or choose cotton or raffia to make a sun hat for the warmer months.

MATERIALS
For wide-brimmed hat (see page 45)
Rico Creative Twist Super Chunky, 80% acrylic, 20% alpaca (82yd/75m per 100g ball), or any super chunky yarn: 2[2:2] x 100g balls in 009 Bordeaux (A)

6.5mm (UK3:USK/10.5) crochet hook

Blunt-ended yarn needle

MATERIALS
For raffia sun hat (see page 47)
Rico Creative Paper, 100% paper fibre (60yd/55m per 50g ball): 2[3:3] x 50g balls in 017 Grey (B)

6mm (UK4:USJ/10) crochet hook

Blunt-ended yarn needle

SIZE
To fit: up to 20[22:24]in (51[56:61]cm) head circumference

TENSION
9 sts and 10 rows to 4in (10cm) over double crochet on 6.5mm hook and A, or 6mm hook and B. Use larger or smaller hook if necessary to obtain correct tension.

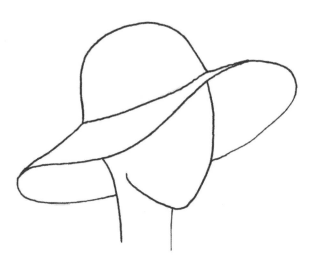

METHOD

The hat is worked in continuous rounds of double crochet throughout. The stitches of the brim are worked into the back loops only and shaped by increasing stitches on every alternate round.

CROWN

Starting at the top of the crown, with 6.5mm hook and A, or 6mm hook and B, make a magic loop (see page 132).

Round 1: 1 ch, 5 dc into loop (5 sts).

Round 2 (inc): (Dc2inc) 5 times (10 sts). Pull tightly on short end of yarn to close loop.

Round 3 (inc): (Dc2inc, 1 dc) 5 times (15 sts).

Round 4 (inc): (Dc2inc, 2 dc) 5 times (20 sts).

Round 5 (inc): (Dc2inc, 3 dc) 5 times (25 sts). Continue increasing 5 sts on each round as set until there are 45[50:55] sts.

Next: 1 dc in each dc without shaping until work measures 6¼[6¾:7¼]in (16[17:18.5]cm) from top of hat.

KEY

↻	magic loop
⌀	chain (ch)
•	slip stitch (sl st)
+	double crochet (dc)
⤬	dc2inc
⋔	double crochet in back loop only
⤬⋔	dc2inc in back loop only

CROWN
Size 20in (51cm)
Rounds 1 to end

CROWN
Size 22in (56cm)
Rounds 1 to end

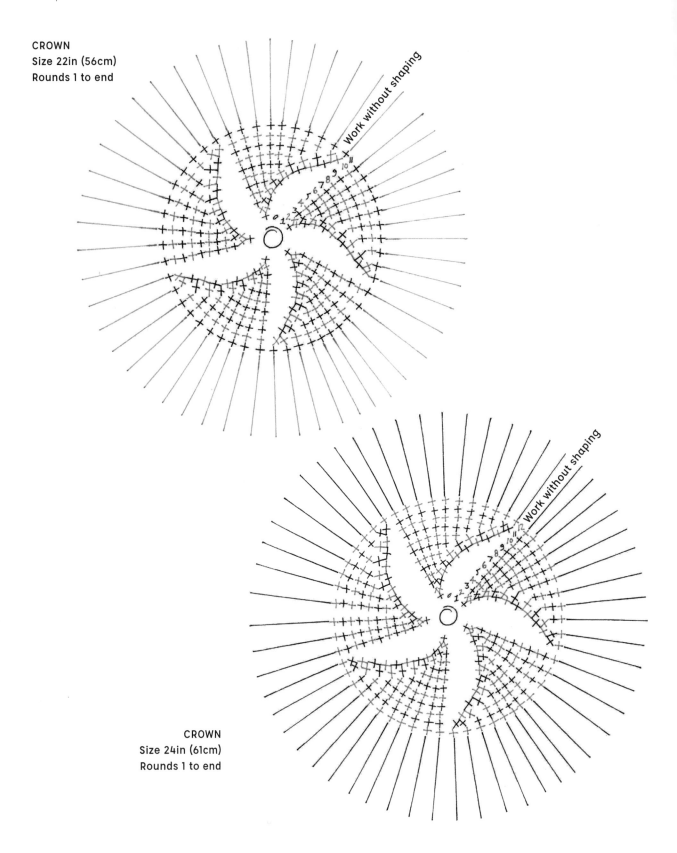

CROWN
Size 24in (61cm)
Rounds 1 to end

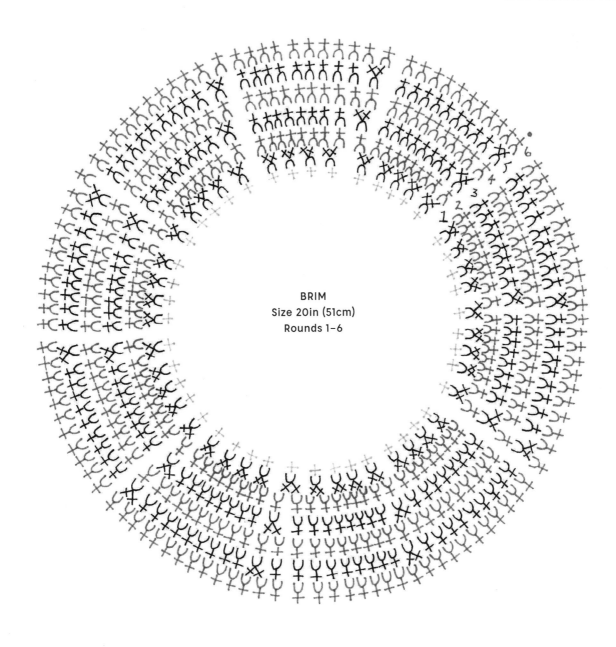

BRIM
Size 20in (51cm)
Rounds 1–6

BRIM

Continue in the back loop only of each dc.

Round 1: (Dc2inc) 45[50:55] times (90[100:110]) sts.

Round 2: 1 dc in each dc.

Round 3 (inc): (Dc2inc, 8[9:10] dc) 10 times (100[110:120] sts).

Round 4: 1 dc in each dc.

Round 5 (inc): (Dc2inc, 9[10:11] dc) 10 times (110[120:130] sts).

Round 6: 1 dc in each dc.

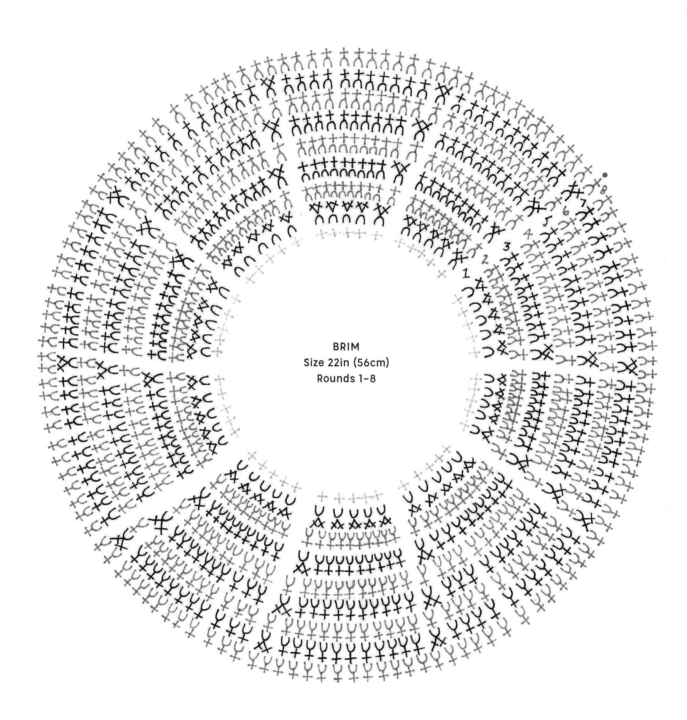

BRIM
Size 22in (56cm)
Rounds 1–8

Sizes 22–24in (56–61cm) only

Round 7 (inc): Increase 10 stitches as set ([130:140] sts).

Round 8: 1 dc in each dc.

All sizes

Sl st in back loop only of next st and fasten off. Weave in yarn ends.

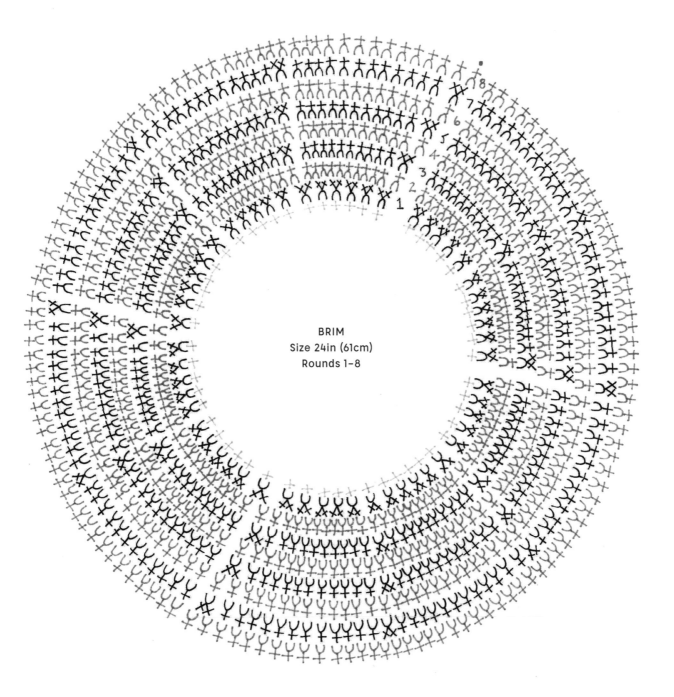

BRIM
Size 24in (61cm)
Rounds 1–8

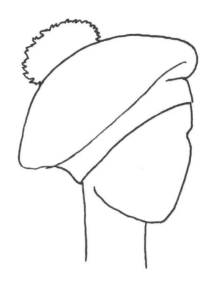

Pompom Tam

This hat is worked entirely in rounds of double crochet. It is finished with a simple decorative band and topped with a large, fluffy pompom.

MATERIALS
Drops Nepal, 65% wool, 35% alpaca (82yd/75m per 50g ball), or any Aran yarn: 2[3:3] x 50g balls in 0500 Light Grey Mix or 8912 Blush (see page 130) (A)

Drops Brushed Alpaca Silk, 77% alpaca, 23% silk (153yd/140m per 25g ball), or any fluffy yarn: 1[1:1] x 25g ball in 02 Light Grey or 08 Heather (see page 130) (B)

5mm (UK6:USH/8) crochet hook

Blunt-ended yarn needle

SIZE
To fit: up to 20[22:24]in (51[56:61]cm) head circumference

TENSION
17 sts and 18 rows to 4in (10cm) over double crochet on 5mm hook. Use larger or smaller hook if necessary to obtain correct tension.

KEY

⟳   magic loop

•   slip stitch (sl st)

⟋   chain (ch)

✛   double crochet (dc)

⤫   dc2inc

⤫   dc2tog

⋔   double crochet in back loop only

METHOD

The hat is worked in rounds of double crochet throughout. The stitches are increased from the centre of the top of the hat, and then decreased after working a number of rounds without shaping. The decorative band of the hat is formed by crocheting into the back loop only of each stitch. The tam is finished with a pompom sewn to the top.

CROWN

Starting at the top of the hat, with 5mm hook and A, make a magic loop (see page 132).

Round 1: 1 ch, 6 dc into loop (6 sts).

Round 2 (inc): (Dc2inc) 6 times (12 sts). Pull tightly on short end of yarn to close loop.

Round 3 (inc): (Dc2inc) 12 times (24 sts).

Round 4 (inc): (Dc2inc, 1 dc) 12 times (36 sts).

Round 5: 1 dc in each dc.

Round 6 (inc): (Dc2inc, 2 dc) 12 times (48 sts).

Round 7: 1 dc in each dc.

Round 8 (inc): (Dc2inc, 3 dc) 12 times (60 sts).

Round 9: 1 dc in each dc.

Rounds 10–18[20:22]: Increase 12 sts on next and every alt round as set until there are 120[132:144] sts.

Next: Work 10[12:14] rounds of 1 dc in each dc.

CROWN
Size 20in (51cm)
Follow rounds 1–28

Sizes 22 & 24in (56 & 61cm)
Follow rounds 1–19 only

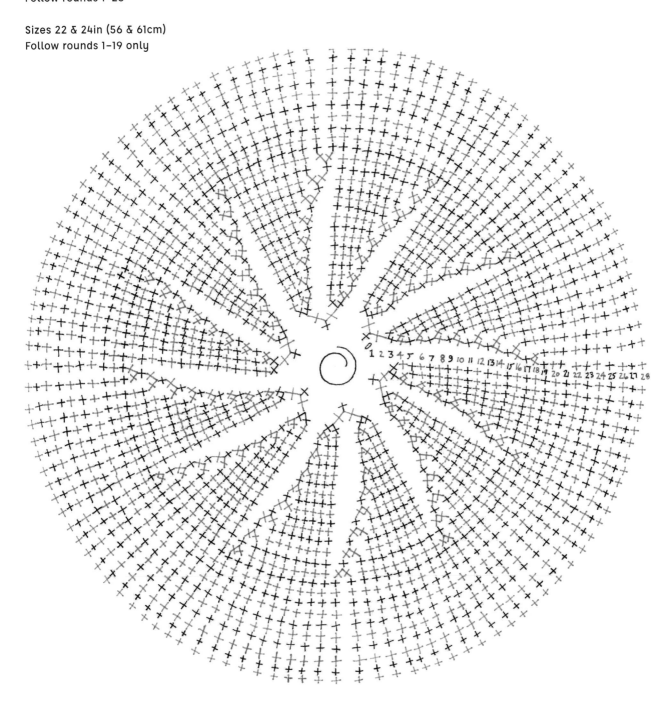

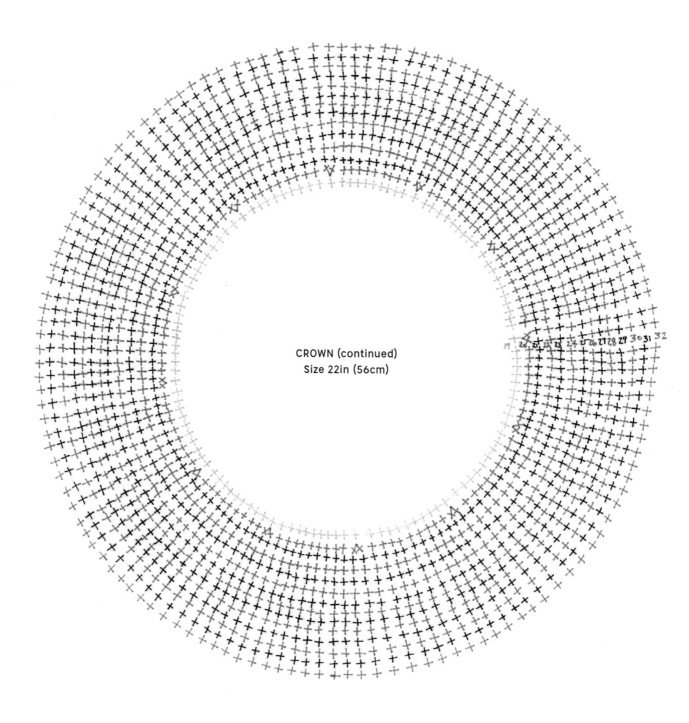

CROWN (continued)
Size 22in (56cm)

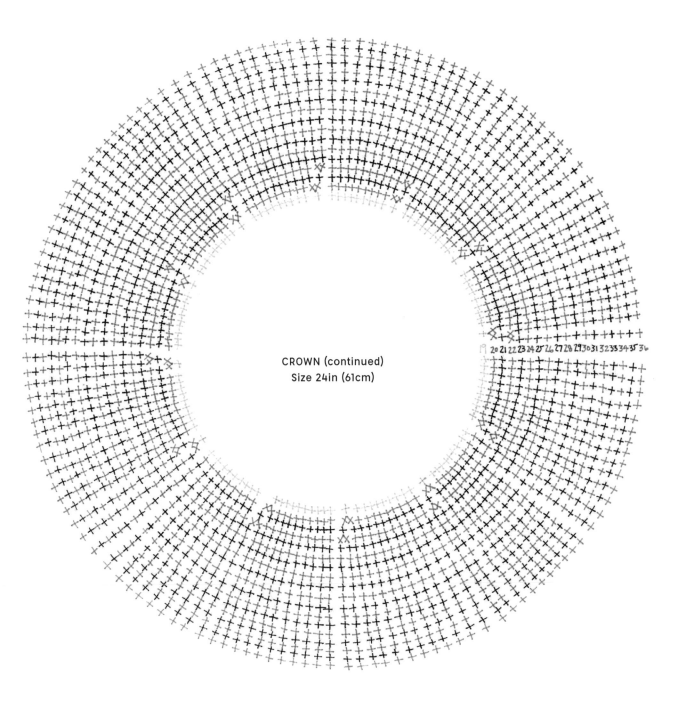

CROWN (continued)
Size 24in (61cm)

SHAPE SIDES

Round 1 (dec): (Dc2tog, 8[9:10] dc) 12 times (108[120:132] sts).

Round 2: 1 dc in each dc.

Round 3 (dec): (Dc2tog, 7[8:9] dc) 12 times (96[108:120] sts).

Round 4: 1 dc in each dc.

Rounds 5–7: Decrease 12 sts on next and every alt round as set until there are 72[84:96] sts.

BAND

Rounds 8–11[12:12]: 1 dc in back loop only of each dc.

Sl st in next dc and fasten off.

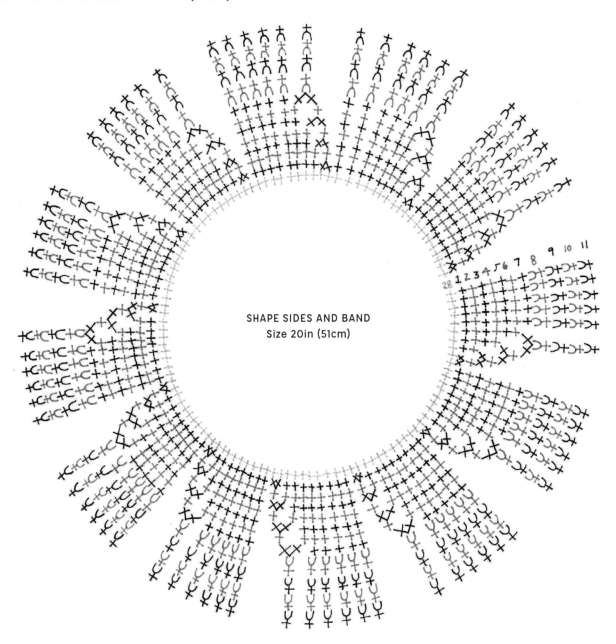

SHAPE SIDES AND BAND
Size 20in (51cm)

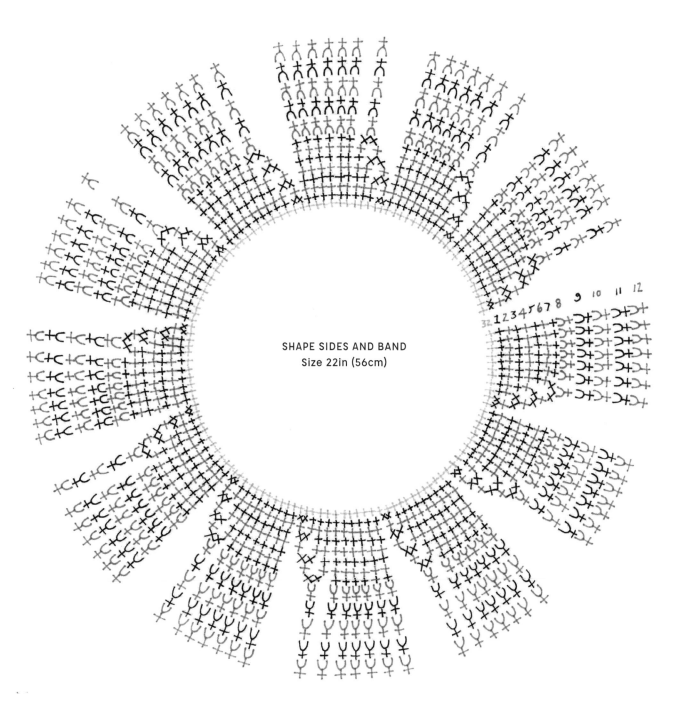

SHAPE SIDES AND BAND
Size 22in (56cm)

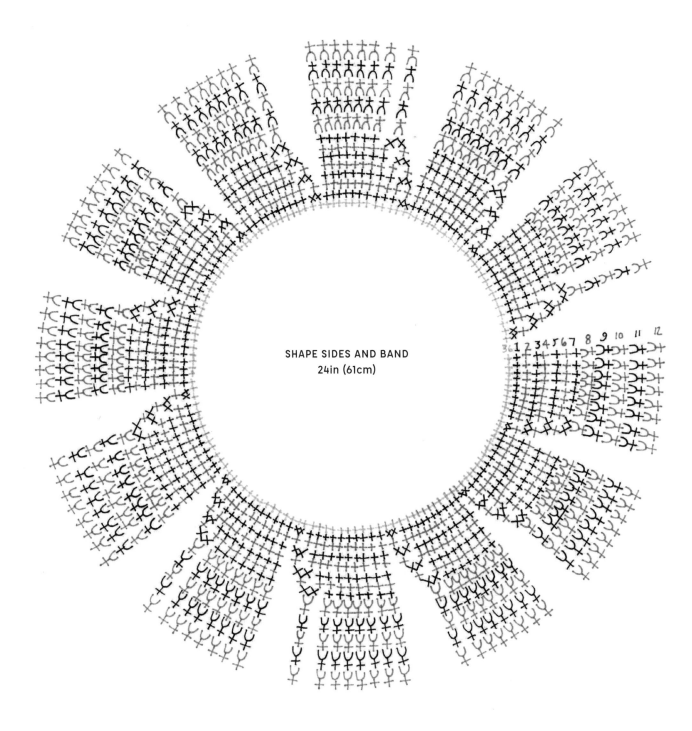

SHAPE SIDES AND BAND
24in (61cm)

MAKING UP

1 To make the pompom, cut two circles of card 2³/₈[2³/₄:3¹/₈]in (6[7:8]cm) in diameter. Make a hole in the centre of each circle. The hole should be around one-third of the size of the circle. Thread a blunt needle with a long length of doubled yarn B and, with the two circles of card together, wind the yarn through the hole and around the outer edge of the circle. Continue in this way, using new lengths of yarn B until the hole is filled and the circle is covered.

2 Cut through the yarn around the outer edge between the two circles of card. Tie a length of yarn B securely around the middle, leaving long ends to attach the pompoms to the hat. Remove the card and trim the pompom, fluffing it into shape. Stitch the pompom to the top of the hat. Weave in all ends.

1

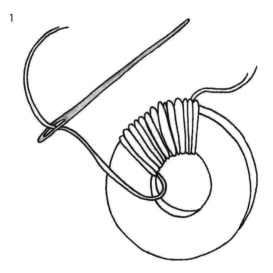

2

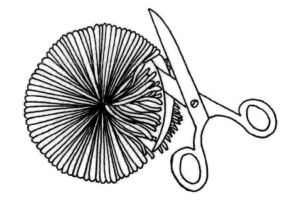

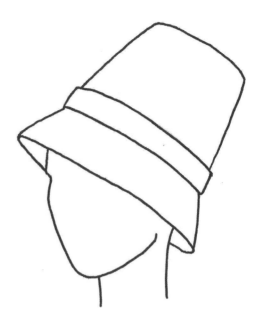

Bucket Hat

The bucket hat has a deep crown and sloping brim. It is crocheted with the yarn doubled to produce a firm fabric. The alpaca blend of the yarn gives the hat a soft, felted texture.

MATERIALS

King Cole Indulge Chunky, 70% acrylic, 9% alpaca, 21% polyester (251yd/230m per 100g ball), or any super chunky yarn:
2[2:2] x 100g balls in 2456 Matador (A)
1[1:1] x 100g ball in 2454 Cardinal (B)

6mm (UK4:USJ/10) crochet hook

Blunt-ended yarn needle

SIZE

To fit: up to 20[22:24]in (51[56:61]cm) head circumference

TENSION

12 sts and 14 rows to 4in (10cm) over double crochet on 6mm hook and yarn A doubled. Use larger or smaller hook if necessary to obtain correct tension.

METHOD

The hat is worked in continuous rounds of double crochet using the yarn doubled. A single round of stitches are worked into the back loops only to help the top of the hat lie flat. A contrasting band completes the bucket hat, crocheted in rows of half treble stitches using a single strand of yarn.

CROWN

Starting at the top of the crown, with 6mm hook and A doubled, make a magic loop (see page 132).

Round 1: 1 ch, 6 dc into loop (6 sts).

Round 2 (inc): (Dc2inc) 6 times (12 sts). Pull tightly on short end of yarn to close loop.

Round 3 (inc): (Dc2inc, 1 dc) 6 times (18 sts).

Round 4 (inc): (Dc2inc, 2 dc) 6 times (24 sts).

Round 5 (inc): (Dc2inc, 3 dc) 6 times (30 sts). Continue increasing 6 sts on each round as set until there are 54[60:66] sts.

Next round: 1 dc in back loop only of each dc.

Next: Work $4^{1}/_{8}$[5:5$^{1}/_{2}$]in (10.5[12.5:14]cm) of 1 dc in both loops of each dc without shaping.

KEY

◯	magic loop
⬭	chain (ch)
•	slip stitch (sl st)
+	double crochet (dc)
✕✕	dc2inc
⌢+	double crochet in back loop only
⊤	half treble (htr)

CROWN
Size 20in (51cm)
Rounds 1–end
Work without shaping

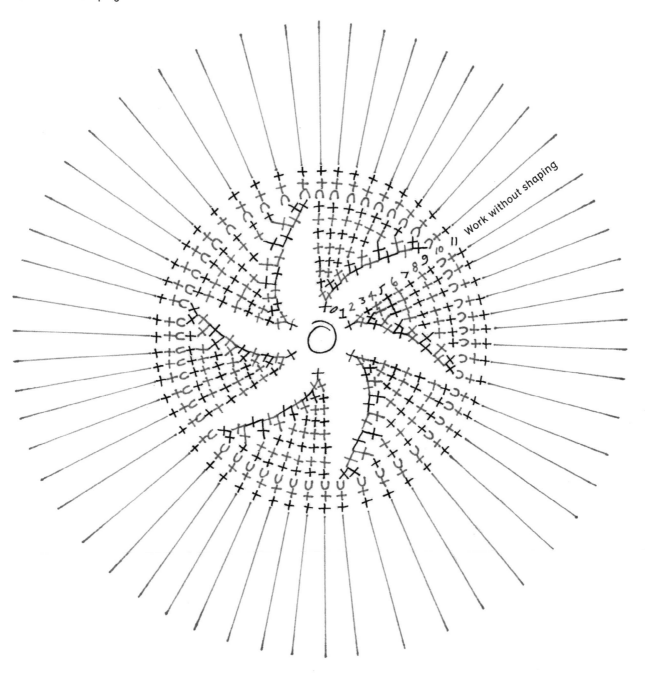

CROWN
Size 22in (56cm)
Rounds 1–end

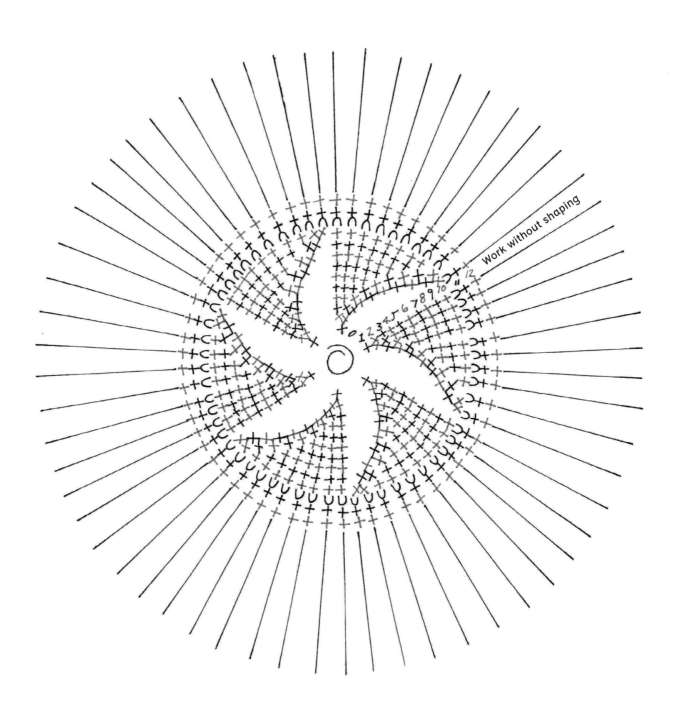

CROWN
Size 24in (61cm)
Rounds 1–end

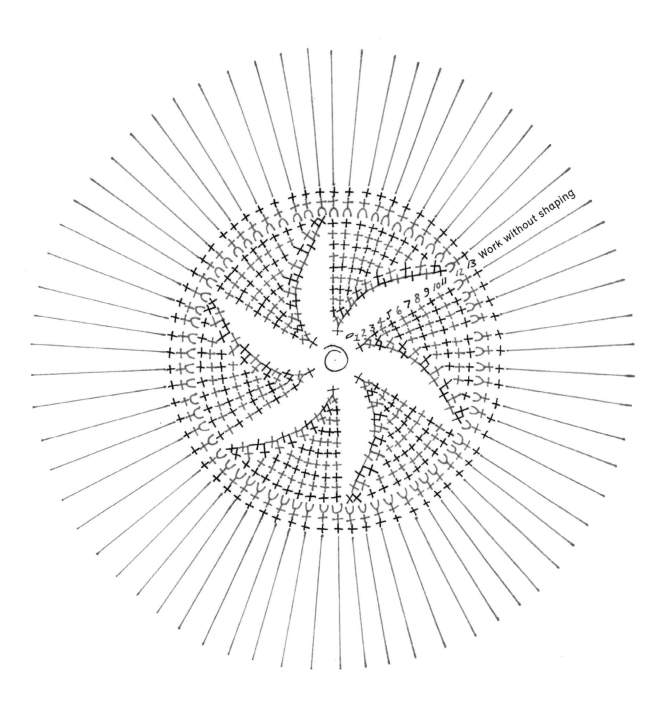

Work without shaping

BRIM

Round 1: (Dc2inc, 1 dc) 27[30:33]
times (81[90:99]) sts.
Rounds 2–5[7:7]: 1 dc in each dc.
Sl st in next st and fasten off.

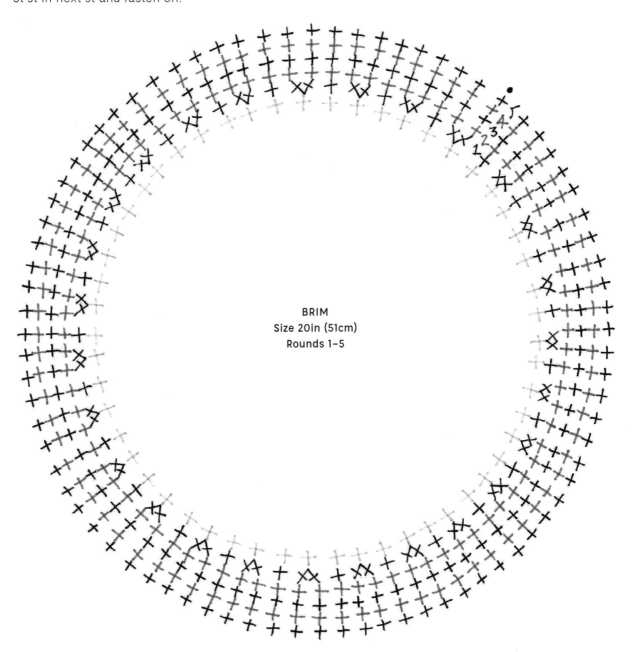

BRIM
Size 20in (51cm)
Rounds 1–5

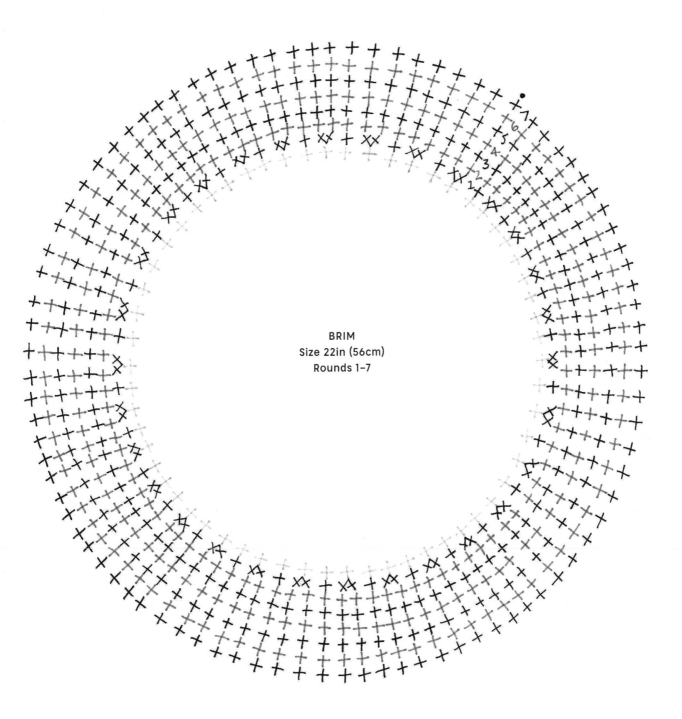

BRIM
Size 22in (56cm)
Rounds 1–7

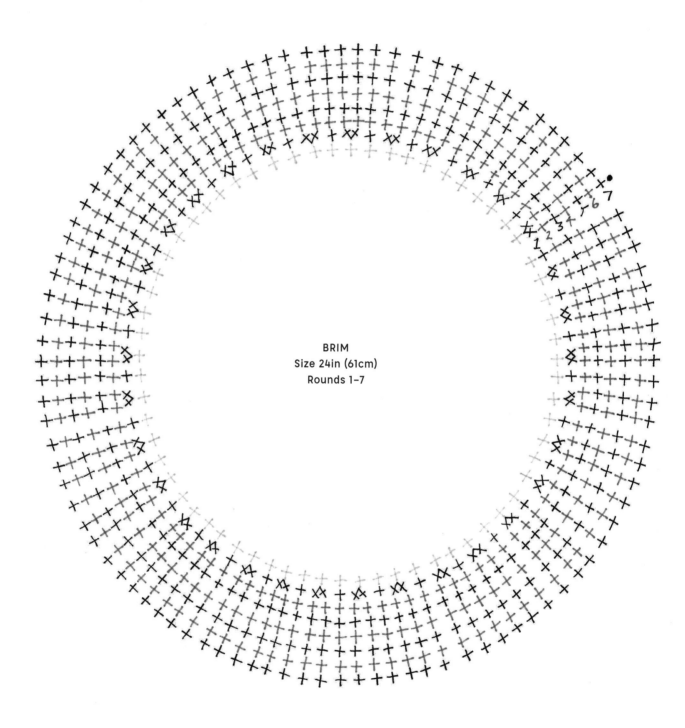

BRIM
Size 24in (61cm)
Rounds 1–7

BAND

With 6mm hook and a single strand of B, make 6[6:6] ch.

Row 1: 1 htr in third ch from hook, 1 htr in next 3[3:3] ch, turn (4[4:4] sts).

Row 2: 2 ch (does not count as a st throughout), 1 htr in each htr to end, turn.

Rep row 2 until band fits around hat. Fasten off, leaving a long tail of yarn.

BAND

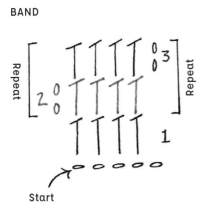

MAKING UP

Wrap the band around the hat and sew together the back seam, working a few stitches through the hat to hold the band in place. Weave in yarn ends.

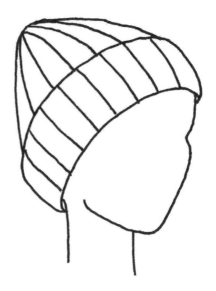

Ribbed Hat

Wear this design as a slouchy hat or with a turned-up edge, as desired.
The rib effect is formed by working into the back loop of each stitch.

MATERIALS
Scheepjes Namaste, 50% wool, 50% acrylic
(92yd/85m per 100g ball), or any chunky yarn:
1[1:2] x 100g balls in 604 Locust, 613 Mountain
or 603 Cobra (see page 130) (A)

8mm (UK0:USL/11) crochet hook

Blunt-ended yarn needle

SIZE
To fit: up to 20[22:24]in (51[56:61]cm)
head circumference

TENSION
12 sts and 8 rows to 4in (10cm) over half treble
on 8mm hook. Use larger or smaller hook if
necessary to obtain correct tension.

METHOD

The hat is worked in rows from side to side. The main part of the hat is crocheted in half treble stitches, and the crown is shaped by working a few double crochet stitches and a slip stitch at the end of alternate rows. The work is turned so the rib is vertical. The stitches at the top of the hat are gathered up, and the edges of the first and last rows are sewn together.

MAIN PIECE

With 8mm hook and A, make 31[33:35] ch.

Row 1: 1 dc in 2nd ch from hook, 1 dc in next 3[3:4] ch, 1 htr in each ch to end, turn (30[32:34] sts).

Row 2: 2 ch (does not count as a st throughout), 1 htr in back loop only of next 26[28:29] htr, 1 dc in back loop only of next 3[3:4] dc, sl st in back loop of next dc, turn.

Row 3: 1 dc in same loop as sl st, 1 dc in back loop only of next 3[3:4] dc, 1 htr in back loop only of each htr to end, turn.

Rep rows 2–3 11[12:13] times more.

Next: Rep row 2 once more. Fasten off, leaving a long tail of yarn at the end.

KEY

- •   slip stitch (sl st)

- ⌀   chain (ch)

- +   double crochet (dc)

- ⋔   slip stitch in back loop only

- ⋔   double crochet in back loop only

- ⋔   half treble (htr) in back loop only

MAKING UP

Thread tail of yarn through stitches at narrow end of the rows, draw up tightly and secure with a few stitches. Sew together the short edges. Weave in all ends. Turn up the brim of the hat.

Size 20in (51cm)

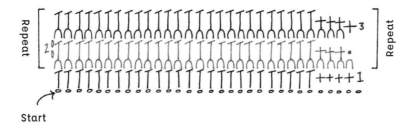

Start

Size 22in (56cm)

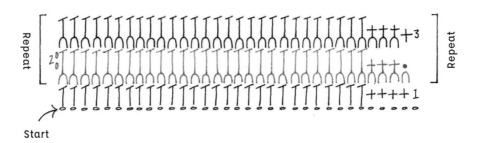

Start

Size 24in (61cm)

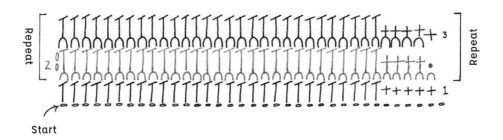

Start

Fairisle Hat with Earflaps

The earflaps and an optional crocheted lining will keep the chill off, making this Nordic-style hat an extra-cosy addition to your winter wardrobe.

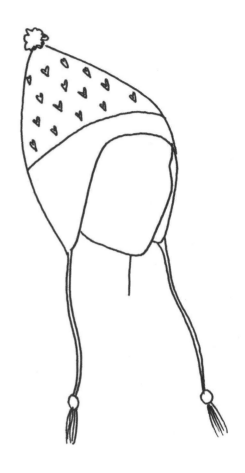

MATERIALS

Drops Alaska, 100% wool (77yd/70m per 50g ball), or any Aran yarn:

With Lining

3[4:5] x 50g balls in 63 Pearl Grey Mix or 53 Ruby Red (A)
2[2:2] x 50g balls in 52 Dark Turquoise or 61 Wheat (B)

Unlined

2[2:3] x 50g balls in 63 Pearl Grey Mix or 53 Ruby Red (A)
2[2:2] x 50g balls in 52 Dark Turquoise or 61 Wheat (B)

5mm (UK6:USH/8) crochet hook

Blunt-ended yarn needle

SIZE

To fit: up to 20[22:24]in (51[56:61]cm) head circumference

Tension

17 sts and 18 rows to 4in (10cm) over double crochet on 5mm hook. Use larger or smaller hook if necessary to obtain correct tension.

METHOD

The hat and lining are worked in double crochet throughout. The top of the hat is worked in continuous rounds, and the border and earflaps are crocheted in rows. The fairisle pattern is created by working the first part of the stitch in the main colour, then finishing the stitch with the contrast colour used for the background. Two rows of double crochet form the edging around the hat. If attaching a lining, the pieces are joined by working the last row of edging into each stitch of both pieces at the same time. Twisted cords and a pompom make the finishing touches.

NOTE

1 ch at beg of the row/round does not count as a st throughout.

LINING

If making an unlined hat, skip to the hat instructions. Starting at the top of the crown, with 5mm hook and A, make a magic loop (see page 132).

Round 1: 1 ch, 5 dc into loop (5 sts).
Round 2 (inc): (Dc2inc) 5 times (10 sts). Pull tightly on short end of yarn to close loop.
Round 3 (inc): (Dc2inc, 1 dc) 5 times (15 sts).
Round 4 (inc): (Dc2inc, 2 dc) 5 times (20 sts).
Round 5 (inc): (Dc2inc, 3 dc) 5 times (25 sts).
Round 6: 1 dc in each dc.
Round 7 (inc): (Dc2inc, 4 dc) 5 times (30 sts).
Round 8 (inc): (Dc2inc, 5 dc) 5 times (35 sts).
Round 9 (inc): (Dc2inc, 6 dc) 5 times (40 sts).
Round 10: 1 dc in each dc.
Round 11 (inc): (Dc2inc, 7 dc) 5 times (45 sts).
Round 12 (inc): (Dc2inc, 8 dc) 5 times (50 sts).
Round 13 (inc): (Dc2inc, 9 dc) 5 times (55 sts).
Round 14: 1 dc in each dc.
Rounds 15–23[27:31]: Increase 5 sts on next and every alternate round until there are 80[90:100] sts.
Next: Work 5 rounds of 1 dc in each dc.

KEY

◯   magic loop

•   slip stitch (sl st)

⌀   chain (ch)

+   double crochet (dc)

⤬⤬   dc2inc

⤬⤬   dc2tog

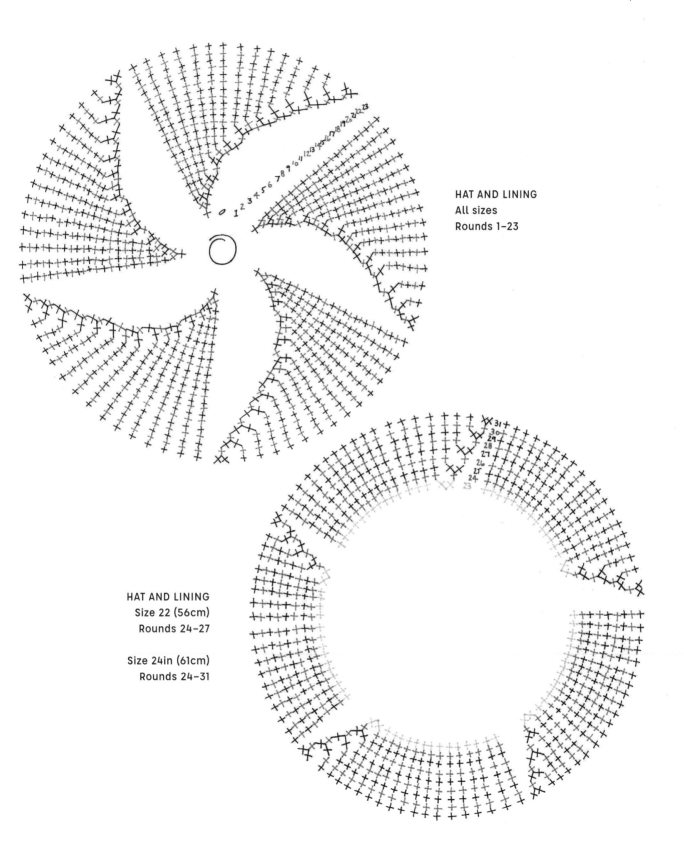

HAT AND LINING
All sizes
Rounds 1–23

HAT AND LINING
Size 22 (56cm)
Rounds 24–27

Size 24in (61cm)
Rounds 24–31

BORDER

Turn work so WS is facing. The
following is worked in rows.
Rows 1–7: 1 ch, 1 dc in each dc,
turn. Fasten off.

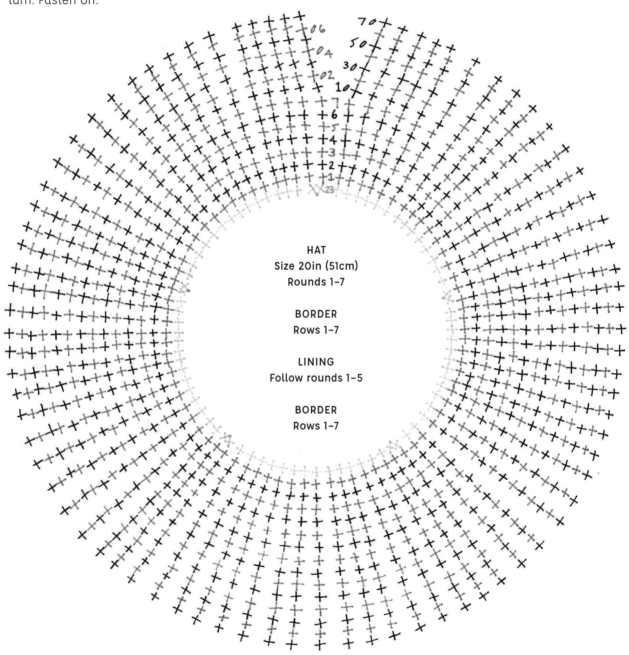

HAT
Size 20in (51cm)
Rounds 1–7

BORDER
Rows 1–7

LINING
Follow rounds 1–5

BORDER
Rows 1–7

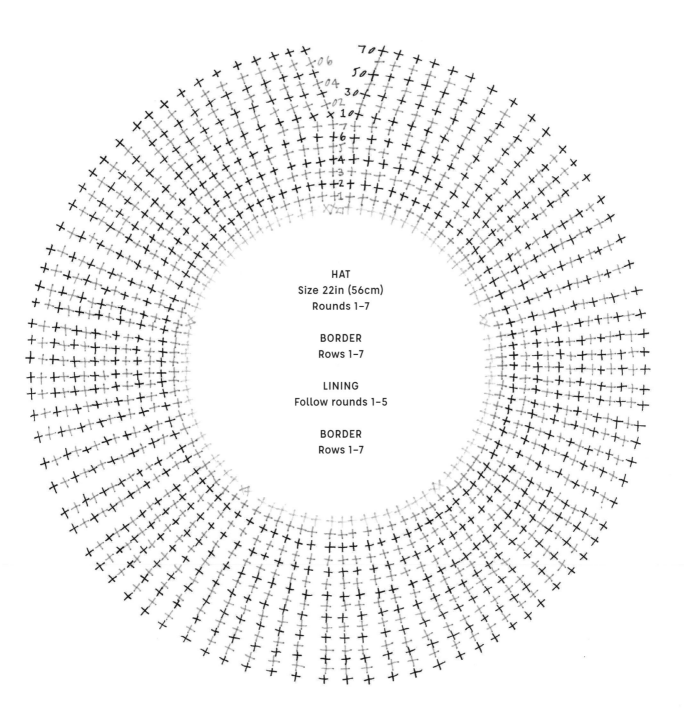

HAT
Size 22in (56cm)
Rounds 1–7

BORDER
Rows 1–7

LINING
Follow rounds 1–5

BORDER
Rows 1–7

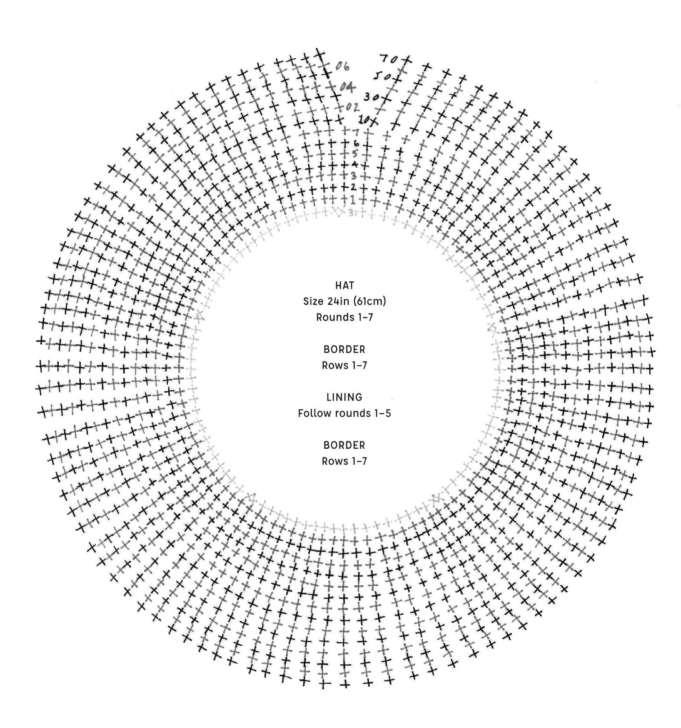

HAT
Size 24in (61cm)
Rounds 1-7

BORDER
Rows 1-7

LINING
Follow rounds 1-5

BORDER
Rows 1-7

FIRST EARFLAP

Turn the work so RS is facing.

Row 1 (RS): Skip first 6[8:9] dc and rejoin A to the next dc with a sl st, 1 dc in same dc as sl st, 1 dc in next 20[22:24] dc, turn.

Continue on these 21[23:25] sts.

Row 2 (WS) (dec): 1 ch, dc2tog, 1 dc in each dc to last 2 sts, dc2tog, turn (19[21:23] sts).

Row 3: 1 ch, 1 dc in each dc to end, turn.

Next: Rep rows 2–3 until 17 sts rem.

Next: Rep row 2 until 3 sts rem. Fasten off.

SECOND EARFLAP

With 5mm hook and RS facing, skip next 26[28:32] sts from first earflap and rejoin A with a sl st to next dc.

Row 1 (RS): 1 dc in same dc as sl st, 1 dc in next 20[22:24] dc, turn.

Continue on these 21[23:25] sts and, starting at row 2, complete to match first earflap.

EDGING

With 5mm hook and RS facing, rejoin A with a sl st to the first dc of the border at the back of the hat.

Next: 1 dc in same dc as sl st, 1 dc in next 5[7:8] sts across the back of the hat, *work 12[14:16] dc evenly down edge of earflap; working in the 3 dc at tip of earflap, dc2inc, 1 dc in next dc, dc2inc, work 12[14:16] dc evenly up edge of earflap*, 1 dc in next 26[28:32] dc across the front of the hat; rep from * to * to finish the edging on the other earflap, 1 dc in next 6[8:9] dc (96[110:124] sts). Fasten off.

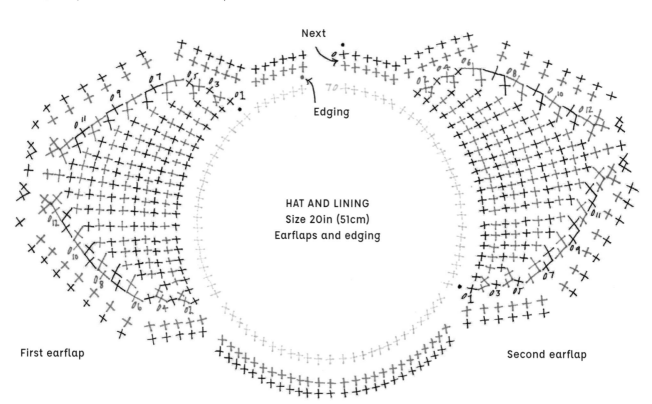

First earflap

Second earflap

HAT AND LINING
Size 20in (51cm)
Earflaps and edging

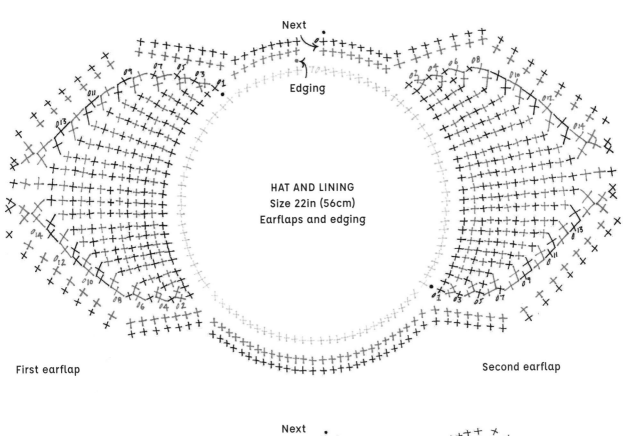

Next

Edging

HAT AND LINING
Size 22in (56cm)
Earflaps and edging

First earflap

Second earflap

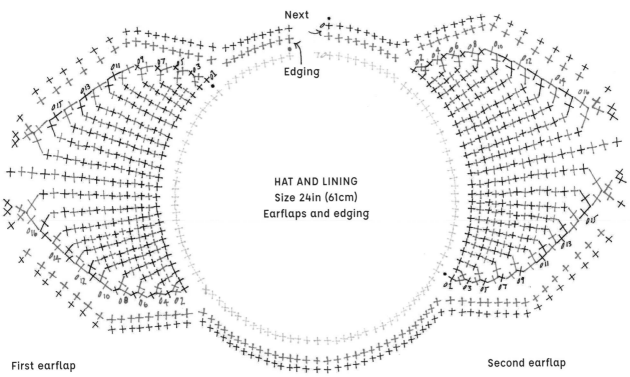

Next

Edging

HAT AND LINING
Size 24in (61cm)
Earflaps and edging

First earflap

Second earflap

HAT

Starting at the top of the crown, with 5mm hook and B, make a magic loop (see page 132).

Rounds 1–5: As rounds 1–5 of lining (25 sts). When working the fairisle pattern, carry unused yarn along the WS of the work.

Round 6: To create the fairisle pattern, (insert hook into next dc, catch yarn A and draw back through st, catch yarn B and draw through both loops to finish dc; with B, work 1 dc in next 4 sts) to end.

Rounds 7–9: As rounds 7–9 of lining (40 sts).

Round 10: Rep fairisle pattern on round 6.

Rounds 11–13: As rounds 11–13 of lining (55 sts).

Round 14: Rep fairisle pattern on round 6.

Rounds 15–23[27:31]: Increase 5 sts on next and each alternate round until there are 80[90:100] sts. **At the same time,** rep fairisle pattern on every fourth round as set.

Next: Work 6[6:7] rounds of 1 dc in each dc, keeping pattern correct.

Next: Work 1[1:0] round of 1 dc in each dc with no fairisle pattern.

BORDER AND EARFLAPS

With yarn A, work as for lining pattern.

EDGING

Work as for the edging on the lining. Do not fasten off, turn.

MAKING UP

If adding lining, slip the lining inside the hat with WS together and work the next row of edging, inserting the hook into the lining and then the corresponding stitch of the hat at the same time to join.

If the hat is unlined, work the next row of edging in each stitch as follows.

Next: With 5mm hook and inside of hat facing, 1 ch, 1 dc in next 19[23:26] dc, dc2inc, 1 dc in next dc, dc2inc, 1 dc in next 52[58:66] dc, dc2inc, 1 dc in next

dc, dc2inc, 1 dc in next 19[23:26] dc, sl st to first dc to join the centre back (100[114:128] sts). Fasten off, leaving a long tail of yarn.

Sew together the openings of the border at the back of the hat and lining.

Cut two circles of card 1¹/₂in (4cm) in diameter. Follow the instructions to make a pompom on page 61 with yarn A and stitch to the top of the hat. Sew a few stitches through to the lining to hold it in place. Weave in all ends.

TWISTED CORDS

1 To make one cord, cut 10 strands of yarn A, each measuring 31[47:47in] (80[120:120]cm) long. Knot the ends of the yarn together. Slip one end over a coat hook and insert a pencil into the other end. Hold the pencil between your thumb and forefinger, keeping the yarn taut. Turn the pencil clockwise to twist the strands.

2 Continue turning the pencil until the strands are tightly twisted. Fold them, allowing the two halves to twist together naturally. Remove the pencil and knot the two ends together before undoing the knots made in the previous step. Trim the ends of yarn to neaten. Sew the other end of the cord to the tip of the earflap.

1
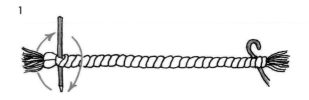

2

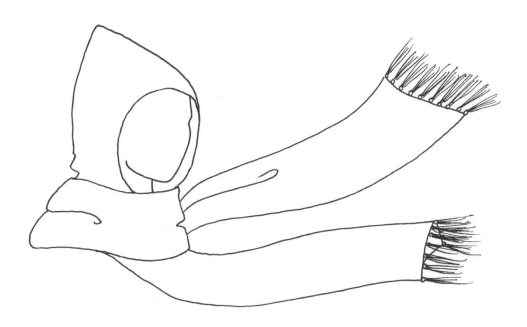

Hooded Scarf

This hood is perfect to keep the chill off your head and neck.
The stitch pattern is similar to the knitted moss or seed stitch.
It is crocheted in rows and finished with a fringe.

MATERIALS
Patons Wool Blend Aran, 63% new wool,
37% acrylic (202yd/185m per 100g ball),
or any Aran yarn: 4[4:5] x 100g balls in
00052 Navy Tweed (A)

5mm (UK6:USH/8) crochet hook

Blunt-ended yarn needle

SIZE
To fit: up to 20[22:24]in (51[56:61]cm)
head circumference

TENSION
18 sts and 16 rows to 4in (10cm) over pattern
on 5mm hook. Use larger or smaller hook if
necessary to obtain correct tension.

METHOD

The hooded scarf is crocheted from one end of the scarf to the other, with the hood formed in the middle. The entire piece is worked in rows of double crochet and chain stitch. The hood is made by increasing with a number of chain stitches at the back of the neck, then worked straight in the same manner as the scarf. The other end of the hood is decreased by ending the row within the same number of stitches that were increased. Then the other end of the scarf is completed. The back seam of the hood is sewn together, and the ends of the scarf are finished with a tasselled fringe.

SCARF: FIRST SIDE

With 5mm hook and A, make 32[40:40] ch.

Row 1: 1 dc in second ch from hook, (1 ch, skip next ch, 1 dc in next ch) to end, turn (31[39:39] sts).

Row 2: 1 ch, (1 dc, 1 ch in next ch sp) to end, 1 dc in turning ch, turn.

Rep row 2 until work measures 15³/₄[29¹/₂:30¹/₄]in (40[75:77]cm).

HOOD

Row 1 (RS) (inc): Make 10[12:16] ch, 1 dc in second ch from hook, (1 ch, skip next ch, 1 dc in next ch) 4[5:7] times, (1 ch, 1 dc in next ch sp) to end, 1 dc in turning ch, turn (41[51:55] sts).

Row 2 (WS): 1 ch, (1 dc, 1 ch in next ch sp) to end, 1 dc in turning ch, turn.

Rep row 2 until hood measures 22¹/₂[24¹/₂:25¹/₂]in (57[62:65]cm), ending with a RS row.

Next (WS): 1 ch, (1 dc in next ch sp, 1 ch) 15[19:19] times, 1 dc in next ch sp, turn.

Continue on these (31[39:39] sts).

SCARF: SECOND SIDE

Work without shaping to match the first side of the scarf.

Follow rows 2–3 of scarf chart, starting with row 3.

KEY:

𝒐   chain (ch)

+   double crochet (dc)

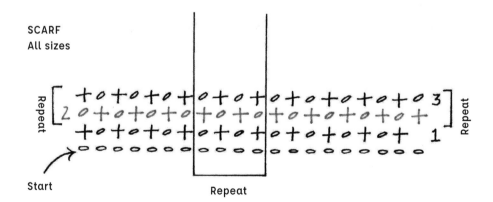

SCARF
All sizes

Repeat

Start

Repeat

Repeat

HOOD
All sizes

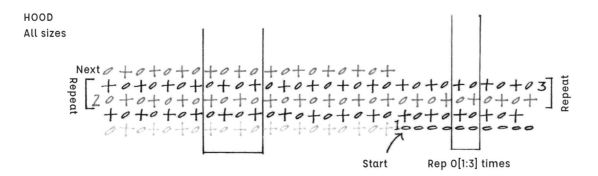

Next

Repeat

2

Start   Rep 0[1:3] times

Repeat

MAKING UP

Fold the work in half, matching the rows. Sew together the back seam of the hood. Weave in all ends.

Fringe

Cut a piece of cardboard 4[6:6]in (10[15:15]cm) long. Wind the yarn around it seven times. Cut through one edge of yarn and fold the lengths in half.

1 Insert the crochet hook into a ch sp at the corner of the end of the scarf, from the back out through to the front. Catch the looped yarn and pull a little way through.

2 Remove hook and thread ends of yarn back through loop, pulling them tight. This completes one tassel.

Skip next ch sp. Attach a tassel to the next and every alt ch sp to end 8[10:10] tassels. Rep to add a fringe to the other end of the scarf. Trim the ends to neaten.

1

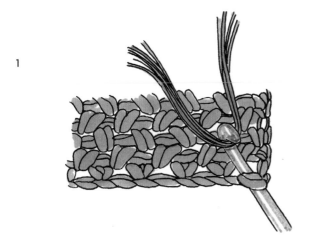

2

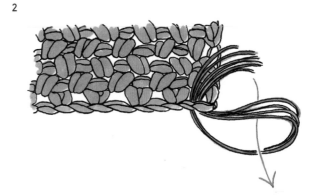

Colourblock Beanie

This beanie has a deep brim, crocheted in blocks of colour. When folded and turned over the hat, it produces a cosy triple layer of fabric.

MATERIALS
Rico Essentials Soft Merino Aran, 100% virgin wool (109yd/100m per 50g ball), or any Aran yarn:
2[2:3] x 50g balls in 095 Mouse Grey (A)
1[1:1] x 50g ball in 063 Lemon (B)
1[1:1] x 50g ball in 097 Anthracite (C)
1[1:1] x 50g ball in 025 Petrol (D)

5mm (UK6:USH/8) crochet hook

Blunt-ended yarn needle

SIZE
To fit: up to 20[22:24]in (51[56:61]cm) head circumference

TENSION
17 sts and 21 rows to 4in (10cm) over double crochet on 5mm hook. Use larger or smaller hook if necessary to obtain correct tension.

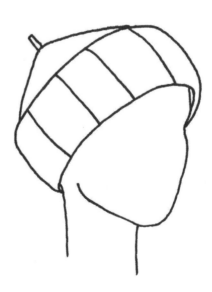

METHOD

The brim is worked in rows of double crochet, from side to side, alternating four colours. The piece is joined by crocheting into the last row and the chain stitches made at the beginning at the same time, to form a ring. The brim is folded in half and the first row of the crown of the hat is crocheted into each stitch along both edges at the same time to join, creating a double layer. The crown is continued in rounds of double crochet, decreasing the stitches towards the top of the hat. A few rounds at the top form a stalk. The end of the yarn is threaded through the tip of the stalk. The reverse side of the crown is the right side, so the hat is turned right side out, and the brim turned up to finish the beanie.

KEY

⌒   chain (ch)

+   double crochet (dc)

✕✕   dc2tog

✚   dc in ch st and dc at same time to join

✚   dc in both sts at same time to join

BRIM

Starting at the side of the brim, with 5mm hook and A, make 37[41:43] ch.
Row 1 (WS): 1 dc in second ch from hook, 1 dc in next 35[39:41] ch, turn (36[40:42] sts).
Rows 2–8[9:10]: 1 ch (does not count as a st throughout), 1 dc in each dc, turn.
Join B in last dc and fasten off A.
Next 9[10:11] rows: With B, work 1 ch, 1 dc in each dc, turn.
Join C in last dc and fasten off B.
Next 8[9:10] rows: With C, work 1 ch, 1 dc in each dc, turn.
Join D in last dc and fasten off C.
Next 9[10:11] rows: With D, work 1 ch, 1 dc in each dc, turn.
These 34[38:42] rows form the striped pattern.
Rows 35[39:43]–102[114:126]: Work 2 more sets of striped pattern.

Join short edges

With RS together fold the piece, aligning the last row of stitches and the chain stitches at the beginning of the brim.
Next: 1 ch, 1 dc in each dc and reverse side of corresponding ch at the same time, to join the short edges. Join A in last dc and fasten off D.

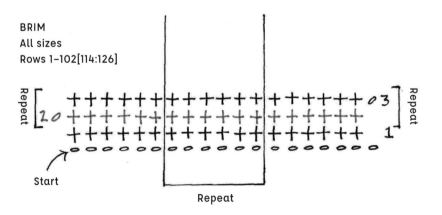

BRIM
All sizes
Rows 1–102[114:126]

BRIM
All sizes
Join short edges

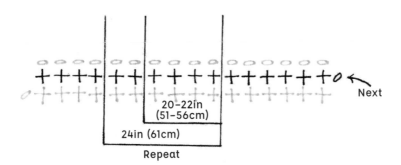

20–22in
(51–56cm)

24in (61cm)

Repeat

Next

CROWN

Fold the piece in half lengthways, with WS together, aligning the edges of the rows of stripes and matching the seam.

Round 1 (WS): 1 ch, work 84[90:102] dc evenly along both edges at the same time to join (84[90:102] sts).

Round 2 (RS) (dec): (Dc2tog, 12[13:15] dc) 6 times (78[84:96]) sts.

Round 3: 1 dc in each dc.

Rep round 3 until work measures 4[4³/₈:4³/₄]in (10[11:12]cm) from beg of crown.

CROWN
Size 20in (51cm)
Round 1

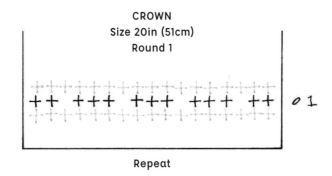

Repeat

CROWN
Size 22in (56cm)
Round 1

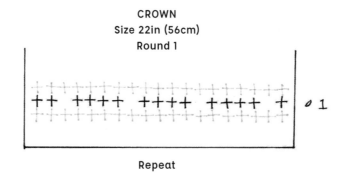

Repeat

CROWN
Size 24in (61cm)
Round 1

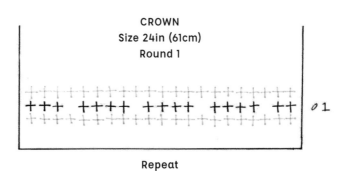

Repeat

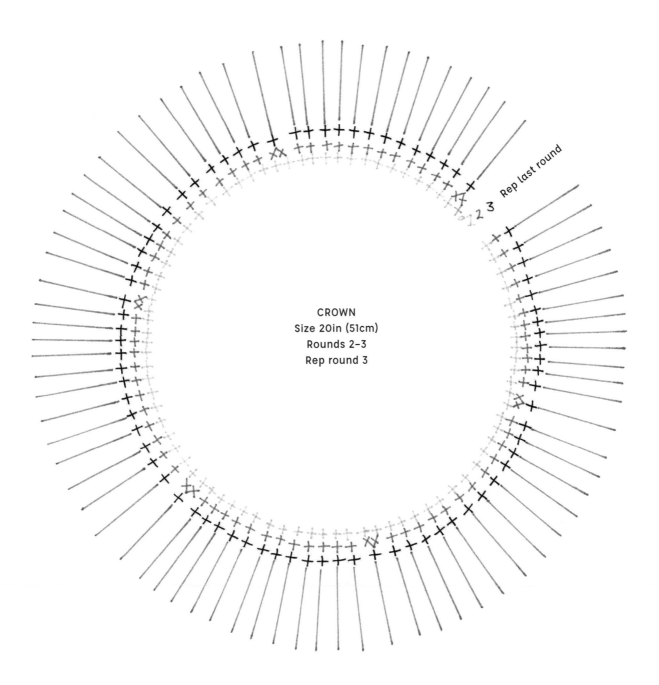

CROWN
Size 20in (51cm)
Rounds 2–3
Rep round 3

Rep last round

2 3

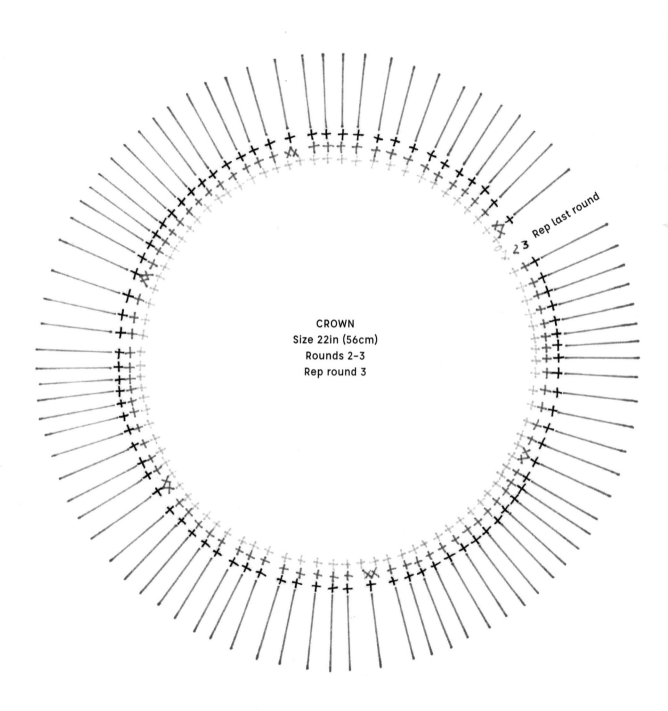

CROWN
Size 22in (56cm)
Rounds 2-3
Rep round 3

Rep last round

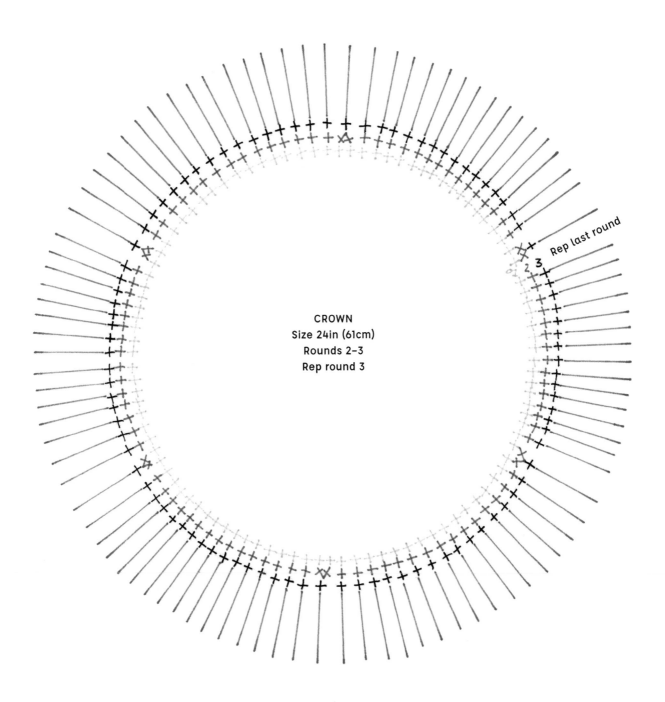

CROWN
Size 24in (61cm)
Rounds 2–3
Rep round 3

Rep last round

3

SHAPE TOP OF CROWN

Round 1 (dec): (Dc2tog, 11[12:14] dc) 6 times (72[78:90]) sts.

Round 2 (dec): (Dc2tog, 10[11:13] dc) 6 times (66[72:84]) sts.

Round 3 (dec): (Dc2tog, 9[10:12] dc) 6 times (60[66:78]) sts.

Rounds 4–12[13:15] (dec): Continue decreasing 6 sts on each round as set until there are 6 sts.
For size 20in (51cm), follow rounds 4-15 of chart.
For size 22in (56cm), follow rounds 3-15 of chart.
For size 24in (61cm), follow rounds 1-15 of chart.

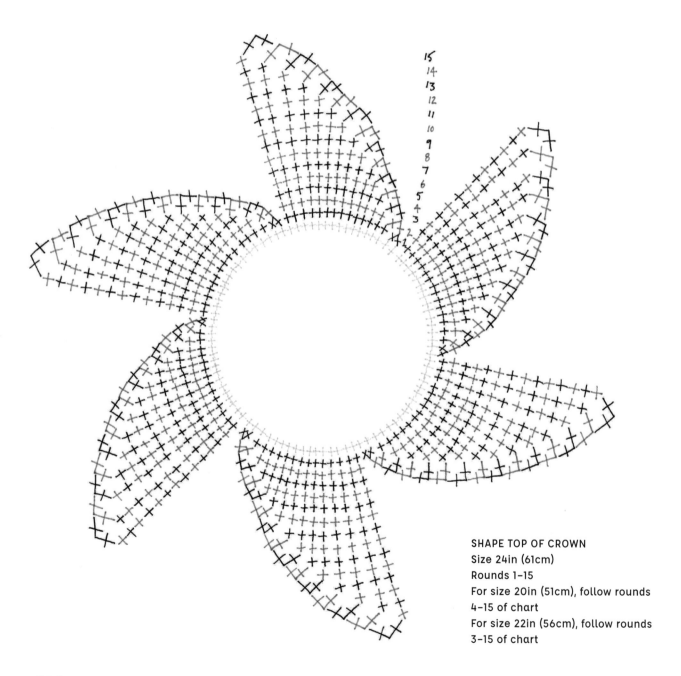

SHAPE TOP OF CROWN
Size 24in (61cm)
Rounds 1-15
For size 20in (51cm), follow rounds
4-15 of chart
For size 22in (56cm), follow rounds
3-15 of chart

STALK

Work 5[5:6] rounds of 1 dc in each dc. Fasten off, leaving a long tail of yarn at the end.

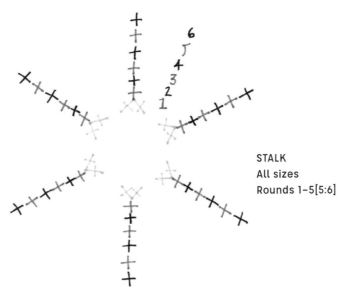

STALK
All sizes
Rounds 1–5[5:6]

MAKING UP

Thread the long tail of yarn left after fastening off through the last round, pull tightly and fasten off. Turn the hat right side out. Weave in all ends. Turn up the brim.

Pinwheel Beret

This beret is worked in continuous rounds of double crochet.
Chain stitch eyelets are staggered on each round to create
the effect of the curving lines of a pinwheel.

MATERIALS
Drops Muskat, 100% cotton (109yd/100m per 50g
ball), or any DK yarn: 2[3:3] x 50g balls in 41
Bordeaux (A)

4mm (UK8:USG/6) crochet hook

Blunt-ended yarn needle

SIZE
To fit: up to 20[22:24]in (51[56:61]cm)
head circumference

TENSION
20 sts and 20 rows to 4in (10cm) over double
crochet on 4mm hook. Use larger or smaller
hook if necessary to obtain correct tension.

METHOD

The beret is worked in continuous rounds throughout. The eyelets are made by working two chain stitches and skipping one double crochet on each round. The hat is increased in the next row by crocheting two stitches into each eyelet. The positioning of the eyelets creates an accentuated curve.

CROWN

Starting at the top of the hat, with 4mm hook and A, make a magic loop (see page 132).

Round 1: 1 ch, 6 dc into loop (6 sts). Pull tightly on short end of yarn to close loop.

Round 2 (inc): (Dc2inc) 6 times (12 sts).

Round 3 (inc): (Dc2inc, 2 ch, skip next dc) 6 times (12 sts and 6 2-ch sp).

Round 4 (inc): (1 dc in next dc, 2 ch, skip next dc, 2 dc in next 2-ch sp) 6 times (18 sts and 6 2-ch sp).

Round 5 (inc): (2 ch, skip next dc, 2 dc in next 2-ch sp, 1 dc in next 2 dc) 6 times (24 sts and 6 2-ch sp).

Round 6 (inc): (2 dc in next 2-ch sp, 1 dc in next 3 dc, 2 ch, skip next dc) 6 times (30 sts and 6 2-ch sp).

Round 7 (inc): (1 dc in next 4 dc, 2 ch, skip next dc, 2 dc in next 2-ch sp) 6 times (36 sts and 6 2-ch sp).

Round 8 (inc): (1 dc in next 3 dc, 2 ch, skip next dc, 2 dc in next 2-ch sp, 1 dc in next 2 dc) 6 times (42 sts and 6 2-ch sp).

Round 9 (inc): (1 dc in next 2 dc, 2 ch, skip next dc, 2 dc in next 2-ch sp, 1 dc in next 4 dc) 6 times (48 sts and 6 2-ch sp).

Round 10 (inc): (1 dc in next dc, 2 ch, skip next dc, 2 dc in next 2-ch sp, 1 dc in next 6 dc) 6 times (54 sts and 6 2-ch sp).

Round 11 (inc): (2 ch, skip next dc, 2 dc in next 2-ch sp, 1 dc in next 8 dc) 6 times (60 sts and 6 2-ch sp).

Round 12 (inc): (2 dc in next 2-ch sp, 1 dc in next 9 dc, 2 ch, skip next dc) 6 times (66 sts and 6 2-ch sp).

Round 13 (inc): (1 dc in next 10 dc, 2 ch, skip next dc, 2 dc in next 2-ch sp) 6 times (72 sts and 6 2-ch sp).

Round 14 (inc): (1 dc in next 9 dc, 2 ch, skip next dc, 2 dc in next 2-ch sp, 1 dc in next 2 dc) 6 times (78 sts and 6 2-ch sp).

Round 15 (inc): (1 dc in next 8 dc, 2 ch, skip next dc, 2 dc in next 2-ch sp, 1 dc in next 4 dc) 6 times (84 sts and 6 2-ch sp).

Round 16 (inc): (1 dc in next 7 dc, 2 ch, skip next dc, 2 dc in next 2-ch sp, 1 dc in next 6 dc) 6 times (90 sts and 6 2-ch sp).

Round 17 (inc): (1 dc in next 6 dc, 2 ch, skip next dc, 2 dc in next 2-ch sp, 1 dc in next 8 dc) 6 times (96 sts and 6 2-ch sp).

Round 18 (inc): (1 dc in next 5 dc, 2 ch, skip next dc, 2 dc in next 2-ch sp, 1 dc in next 10 dc) 6 times (102 sts and 6 2-ch sp).

Round 19 (inc): (1 dc in next 4 dc, 2 ch, skip next dc, 2 dc in next 2-ch sp, 1 dc in next 12 dc) 6 times (108 sts and 6 2-ch sp).

Round 20 (inc): (1 dc in next 3 dc, 2 ch, skip next dc, 2 dc in next 2-ch sp, 1 dc in next 14 dc) 6 times (114 sts and 6 2-ch sp).

Round 21 (inc): (1 dc in next 2 dc, 2 ch, skip next dc, 2 dc in next 2-ch sp, 1 dc in next 16 dc) 6 times (120 sts and 6 2-ch sp).

Round 22 (inc): (1 dc in next dc, 2 ch, skip next dc, 2 dc in next 2-ch sp, 1 dc in next 18 dc) 6 times (126 sts and 6 2-ch sp).

Round 23 (inc): (2 ch, skip next dc, 2 dc in next 2-ch sp, 1 dc in next 20 dc) 6 times (132 sts and 6 2-ch sp).

Round 24 (inc): (2 dc in next 2-ch sp, 1 dc in next 21 dc, 2 ch, skip next dc) 6 times (138 sts and 6 2-ch sp).

CROWN
All sizes
Rounds 1–24

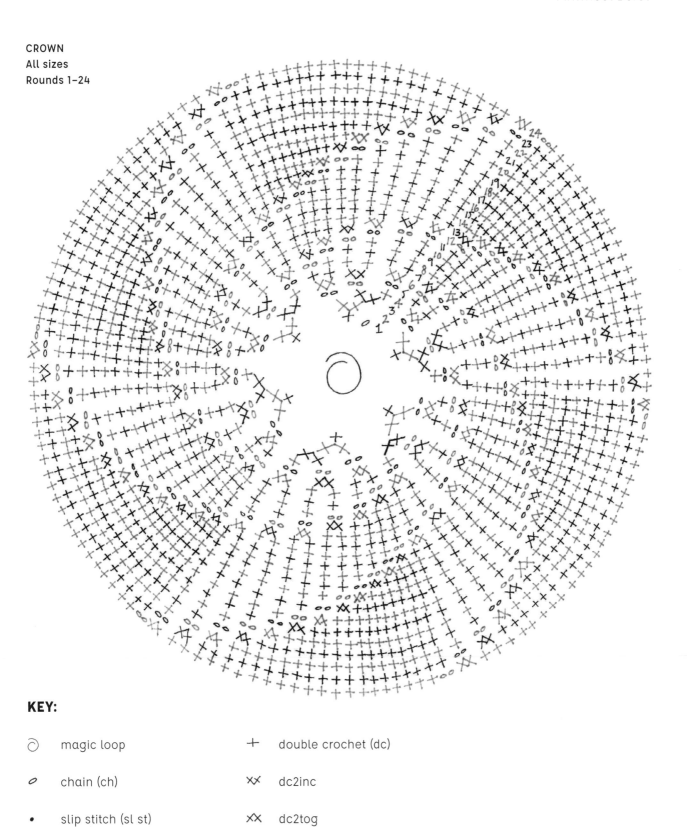

KEY:

⊙	magic loop	+	double crochet (dc)
ᴑ	chain (ch)	⋋⋌	dc2inc
•	slip stitch (sl st)	⋎⋏	dc2tog

CROWN (continued)
Size 20in (51cm)
Rounds 25–27

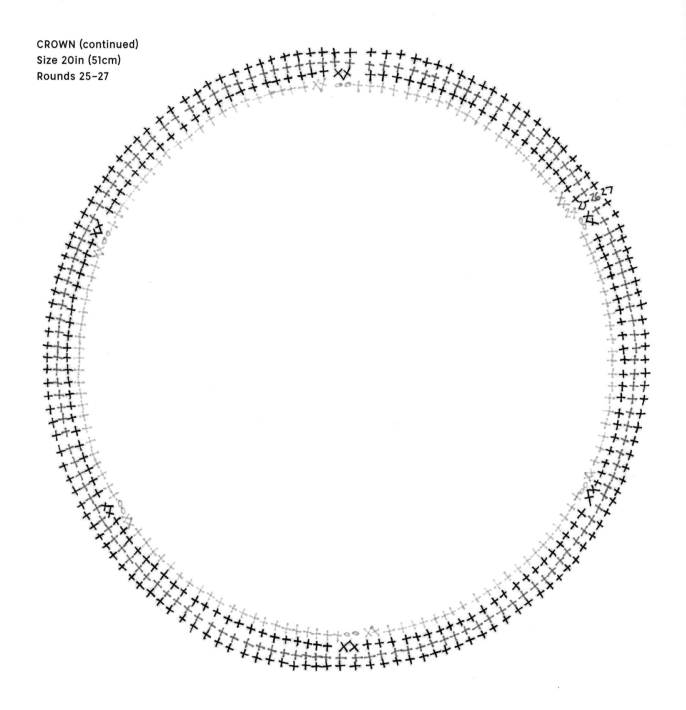

Size 20in (51cm) only
Round 25 (inc): (1 dc in next 22 dc, skip next dc,
2 dc in next 2-ch sp) 6 times (144 sts).
Rounds 26–27: 1 dc in each dc.

CROWN (continued)
Size 22in (56cm)
Rounds 25–29

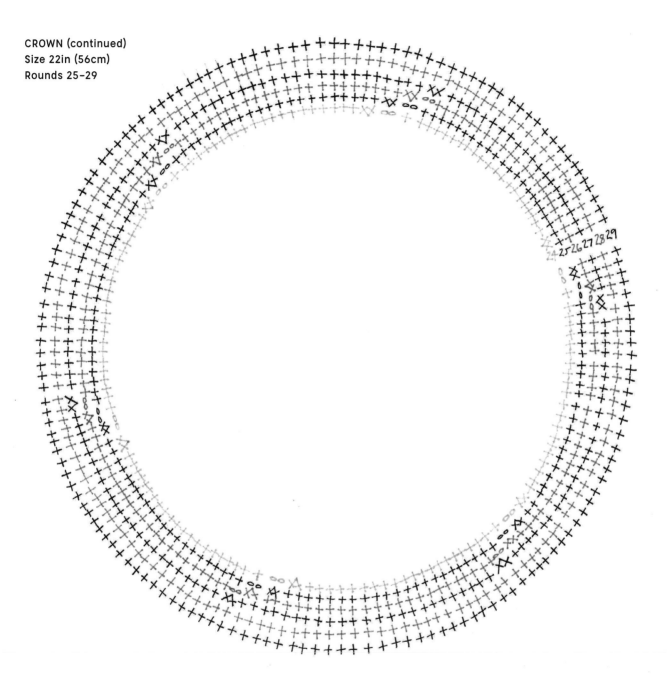

24 25 26 27 28 29

Sizes 22–24 (56–61cm)

Round 25 (inc): (1 dc in next 22 dc, 2 ch, skip next dc, 2 dc in next 2-ch sp) 6 times (144 sts and 6 2-ch sp).

Round 26 (inc): (1 dc in next 21 dc, 2 ch, skip next dc, 2 dc in next 2-ch sp, 1 dc in next 2 dc) 6 times (150 sts and 6 2-ch sp).

Size 22in (56cm) only

Round 27 (inc): (1 dc in next 20 dc, skip next dc, 2 dc in next 2-ch sp, 1 dc in next 4 dc) 6 times (156 sts).

Rounds 28–29: 1 dc in each dc.

CROWN (continued)
Size 24in (61cm)
Rounds 25–31

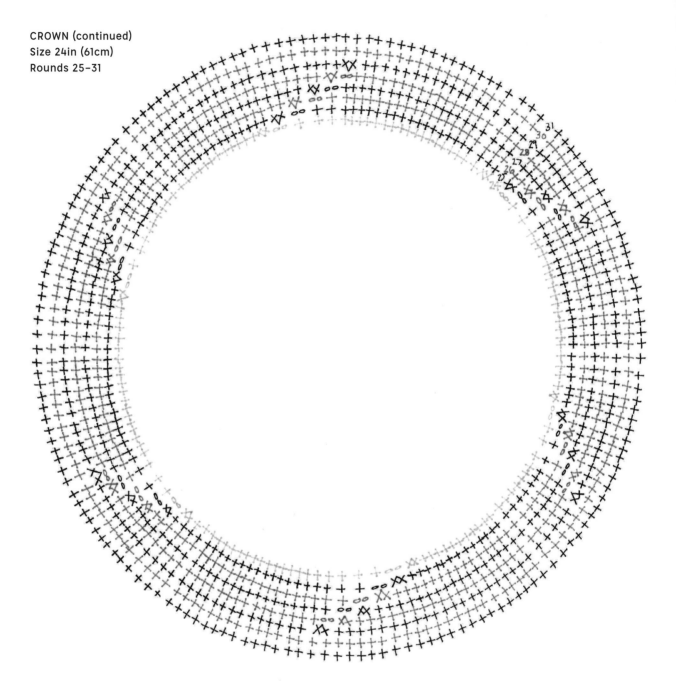

Size 24in (61cm) only

Round 27 (inc): (1 dc in next 20 dc, 2 ch, skip next dc, 2 dc in next 2-ch sp, 1 dc in next 4 dc) 6 times (156 sts and 6 2-ch sp).

Round 28 (inc): (1 dc in next 19 dc, 2 ch, skip next dc, 2 dc in next 2-ch sp, 1 dc in next 6 dc) 6 times (162 sts and 6 2-ch sp).

Round 29 (inc): (1 dc in next 18 dc, skip next dc, 2 dc in next 2-ch sp, 1 dc in next 8 dc) 6 times (168 sts).

Rounds 30–31: 1 dc in each dc.

SHAPE SIDES (ALL SIZES)

Round 1 (dec): (Dc2tog, 10[11:12] dc) 12 times (132[144:156] sts).

Round 2: 1 dc in each dc.

Round 3 (dec): (Dc2tog, 9[10:11] dc) 12 times (120[132:144] sts).

Round 4: 1 dc in each dc.

Round 5 (dec): (Dc2tog, 8[9:10] dc) 12 times (108[120:132] sts).

Round 6: 1 dc in each dc.

Rounds 7–9: Continue decreasing 12 sts on next and every alt round as set until there are 84[96:108] sts.

BAND

Rounds 10–14: 1 dc in each dc.
Sl st in next dc and fasten off.
Weave in all ends.

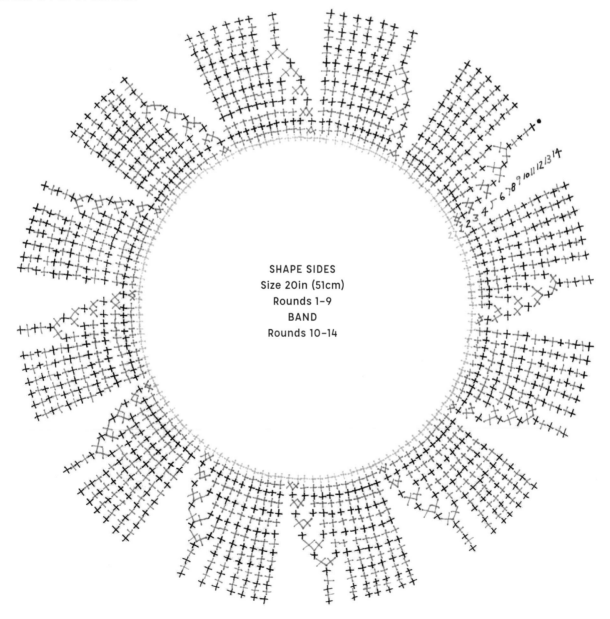

SHAPE SIDES
Size 20in (51cm)
Rounds 1–9
BAND
Rounds 10–14

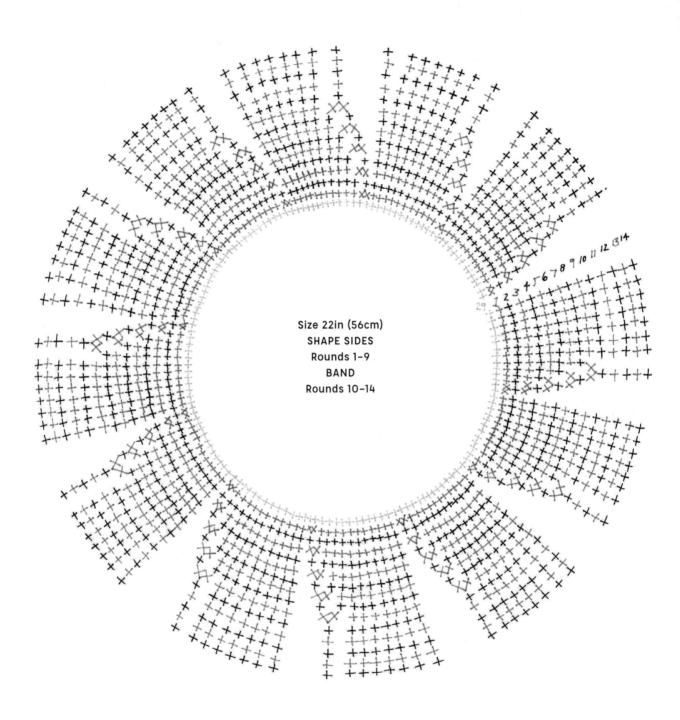

Size 22in (56cm)
SHAPE SIDES
Rounds 1–9
BAND
Rounds 10–14

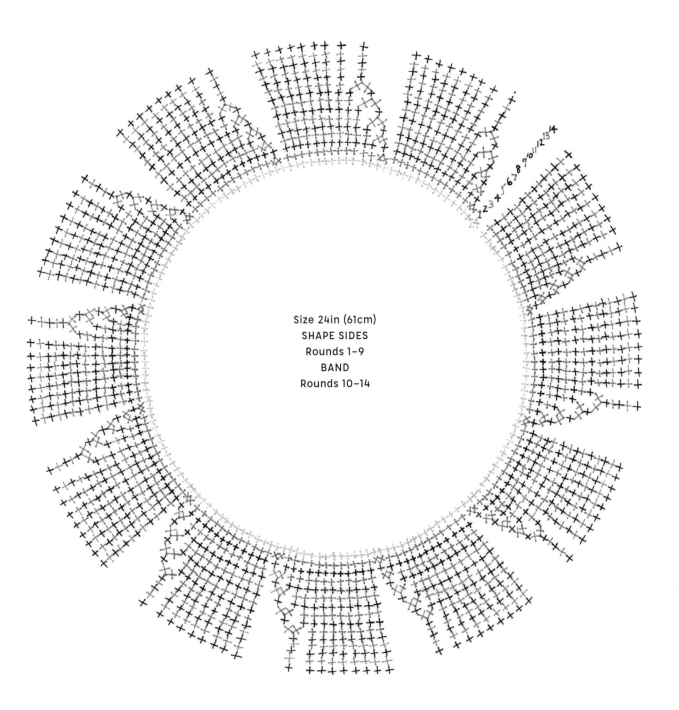

Size 24in (61cm)
SHAPE SIDES
Rounds 1-9
BAND
Rounds 10-14

Bowler Hat

This soft version of a bowler hat is worked entirely in double crochet stitch. It features a curled brim and a band around the crown, finished with a decorative buckle.

MATERIALS
Scheepjes Skies Heavy, 100% premium blend cotton (186yd/170m per 100g ball), or any Aran yarn:
1[1:2] x 100g balls in 105 Stratus (A)
1[1:1] x 100g ball in 106 Cirrostratus (B)

4.5mm (UK7:US7) crochet hook

Buckle with an interior width of ³/₄[1:1¹/₈]in (2[2.5:3]cm)

Blunt-ended yarn needle

SIZE
To fit: up to 20[22:24]in (51[56:61]cm) head circumference

TENSION
18 sts and 18 rows to 4in (10cm) over double crochet on 4.5mm hook and yarn A. Use larger or smaller hook if necessary to obtain correct tension.

CROWN
Size 20in (51cm)
Rounds 1 to end
Sizes 22–24in (56–61cm)
Rounds 1–14

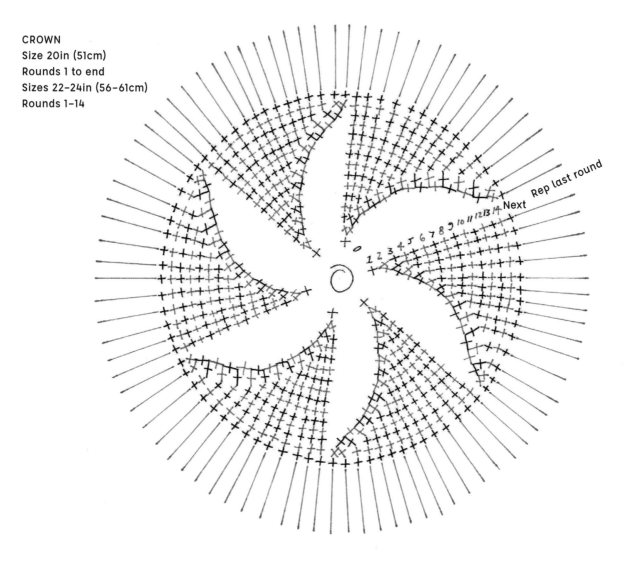

Rep last round

Next

0 1 2 3 4 5 6 7 8 9 10 11 12 13 14

METHOD

The hat itself is worked in continuous rounds, and the band around the crown is in rows of double crochet. The edge of the brim and the band are crocheted in a different shade of yarn. After the first round of increasing the stitches, the brim is crocheted without further shaping to produce the curled edge.

CROWN

Starting at the top of the crown, with 4.5mm hook and A, make a magic loop (see page 132).

Round 1: 1 ch, 6 dc into loop (6 sts).

Round 2 (inc): (Dc2inc) 6 times (12 sts). Pull tightly on short end of yarn to close loop.

Round 3 (inc): (Dc2inc, 1 dc) 6 times (18 sts).

Round 4 (inc): (Dc2inc, 2 dc) 6 times (24 sts).

Round 5 (inc): (Dc2inc, 3 dc) 6 times (30 sts).

Continue increasing 6 sts on each round as set until there are 84[90:102] sts.

Next: 1 dc in each dc without shaping until work measures 6³/4[7:7³/4]in (17[18:19.5]cm) from top of hat.

KEY:

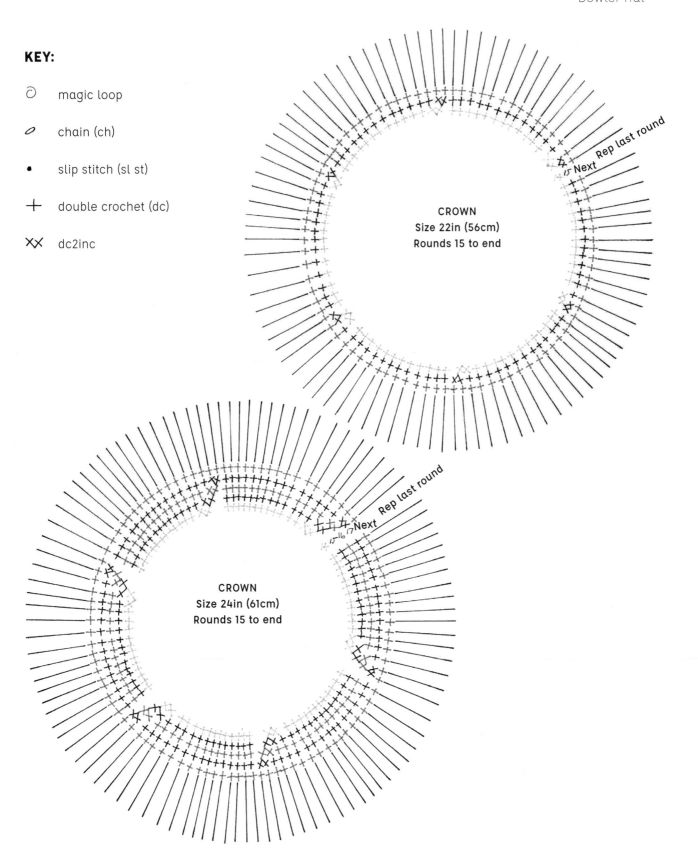

- ◯ magic loop
- ◯ chain (ch)
- • slip stitch (sl st)
- ✛ double crochet (dc)
- ✕✕ dc2inc

CROWN
Size 22in (56cm)
Rounds 15 to end

CROWN
Size 24in (61cm)
Rounds 15 to end

BRIM

Round 1 (RS) (inc): (Dc2inc, 1 dc) 42[45:51] times (126[135:153] sts).

Rounds 2–5[6:7]: 1 dc in each dc. Join B in last dc, sl st in next dc, turn.

Continue in B.

Round 6[7:8] (WS): 1 dc in same st as sl st, 1 dc in each dc to end.

Next (WS): Work 2 rounds of 1 dc in each dc. Sl st in next st and fasten off.

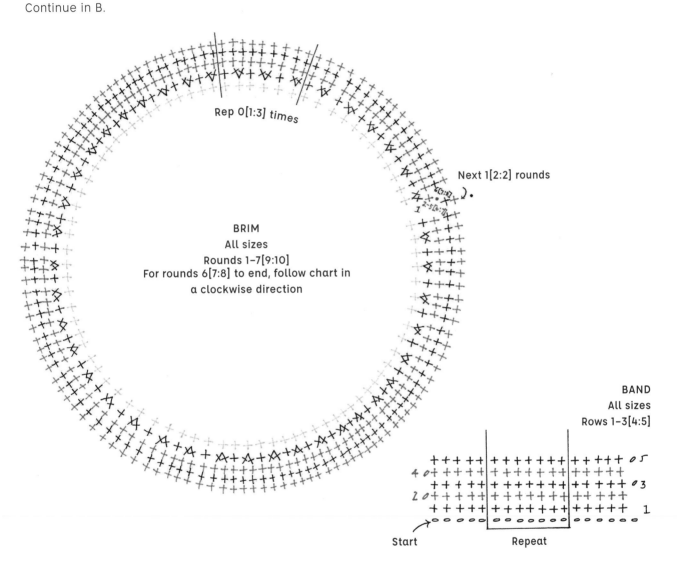

Rep 0[1:3] times

Next 1[2:2] rounds

BRIM
All sizes
Rounds 1–7[9:10]
For rounds 6[7:8] to end, follow chart in a clockwise direction

BAND
All sizes
Rows 1–3[4:5]

Start   Repeat

BAND

With 4.5mm hook and B, make 95[101:113] ch.

Row 1: 1 dc in second ch from hook, 1 dc in each ch to end, turn (94[100:112] sts).

Rows 2–3[4:5]: 1 ch (does not count as a st throughout), 1 dc in each dc to end, turn.

MAKING UP

Slip one end of the band through the buckle. Wrap the band around the hat and sew together the back seam, working a few stitches through the hat to hold the band in place. Weave in yarn ends.

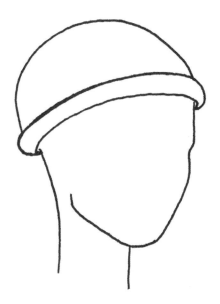

Beanie with Rolled Brim

This beanie is a short style, designed to sit above the ears. If preferred, it can be made longer by adding more rounds before starting the brim.

MATERIALS
Lopi Álafosslopi, 100% wool (109yd/100m per 100g ball), or any chunky yarn: 1[1:1] x 100g ball in 9972 Ecru Heather, 1234 Blue Tweed (see page 7) or 1232 Arctic Exposure (see page 130) (A)

5.5mm (UK5:USI/9) and 6.5mm (UK3:USK/10.5) crochet hooks

Blunt-ended yarn needle

SIZE
To fit: up to 20[22:24]in (51[56:61]cm) head circumference

TENSION
12 sts and 13 rows to 4in (10cm) over double crochet on 5.5mm hook. Use larger or smaller hook if necessary to obtain correct tension.

METHOD

The hat is worked in continuous rounds of double crochet throughout. The last few rounds are worked using a larger hook so the fabric rolls up naturally. The smaller hook is then used for the final round and to anchor the brim to the hat with a slip stitch at regular intervals.

NOTE

To slip stitch around post of stitch, insert hook from RS of work into the gap before the stitch, around the back of the stitch and through the next gap to the front of the work (see illustration); yrh, draw through gaps and loop on hook to finish the slip stitch.

CROWN

Starting at the top of the crown, with 5.5mm hook and A, make a magic loop (see page 132).

Round 1: 1 ch, 6 dc into loop (6 sts).

Round 2 (inc): (Dc2inc) 6 times (12 sts). Pull tightly on short end of yarn to close loop.

Round 3 (inc): (Dc2inc, 1 dc) 6 times (18 sts).

Round 4 (inc): (Dc2inc, 2 dc) 6 times (24 sts).

Round 5 (inc): (Dc2inc, 3 dc) 6 times (30 sts). Continue increasing 6 sts on each round as set until there are 54[60:66] sts.

Next: 1 dc in each dc without shaping until work measures 6³/₄[7:7³/₄]in (17:[18:19.5]cm) from top of hat.

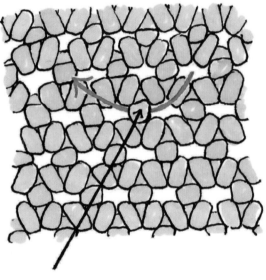

Post of stitch

KEY

⌒   magic loop

𝑜   chain (ch)

•   slip stitch (sl st)

+   double crochet (dc)

✕✕   dc2inc

↺   slip stitch around post of stitch

BRIM

Change to 6.5mm hook and work 3 rounds of
1 dc in each dc.

Next: Change to 5.5mm hook and work (1 dc in
next 9[10:11] dc, sl st around post of st 4 rounds
below to catch brim to hat) 6 times. Fasten off
and weave in yarn ends.

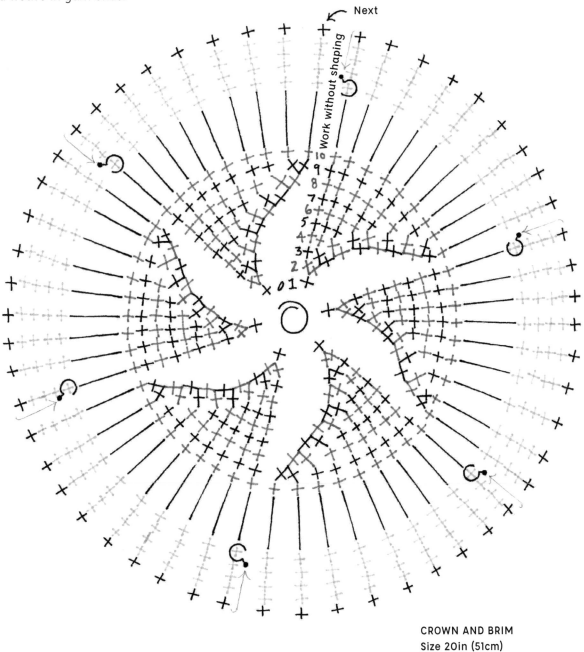

CROWN AND BRIM
Size 20in (51cm)

CROWN AND BRIM
Size 22in (56cm)

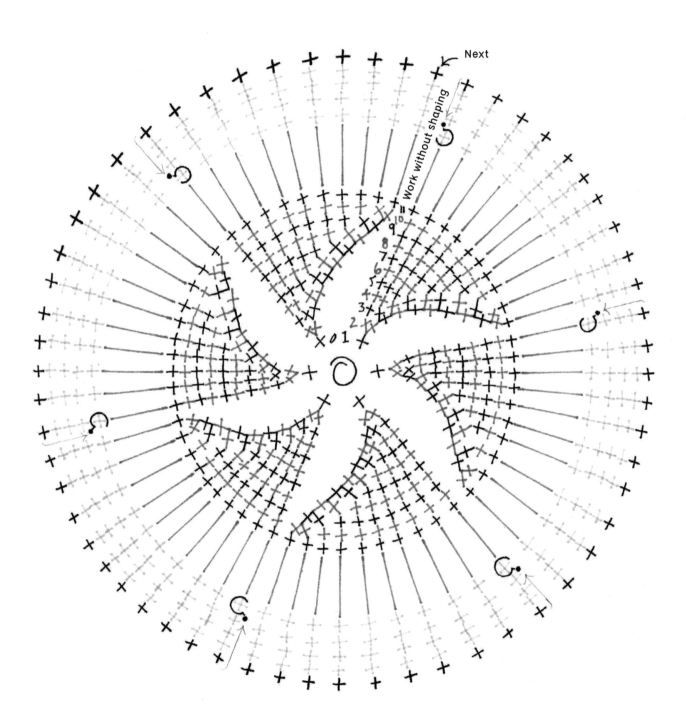

CROWN AND BRIM
Size 24in (61cm)

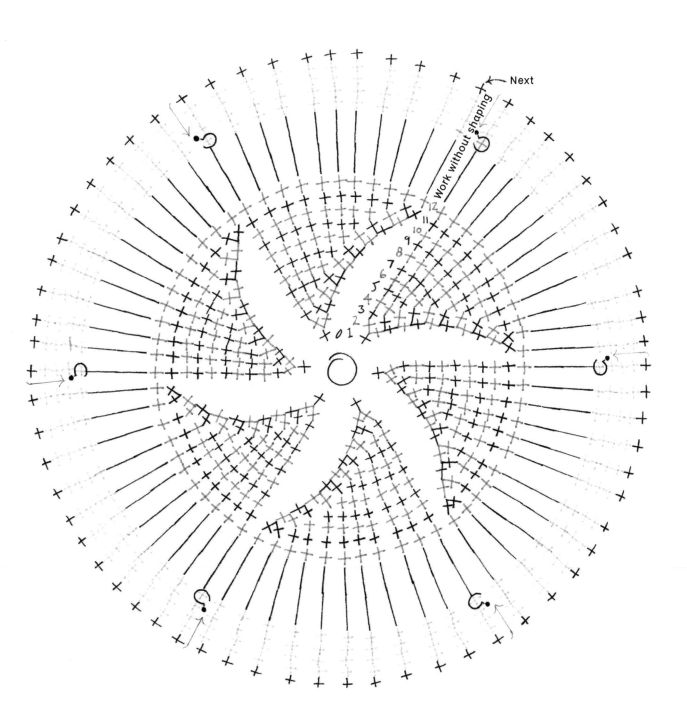

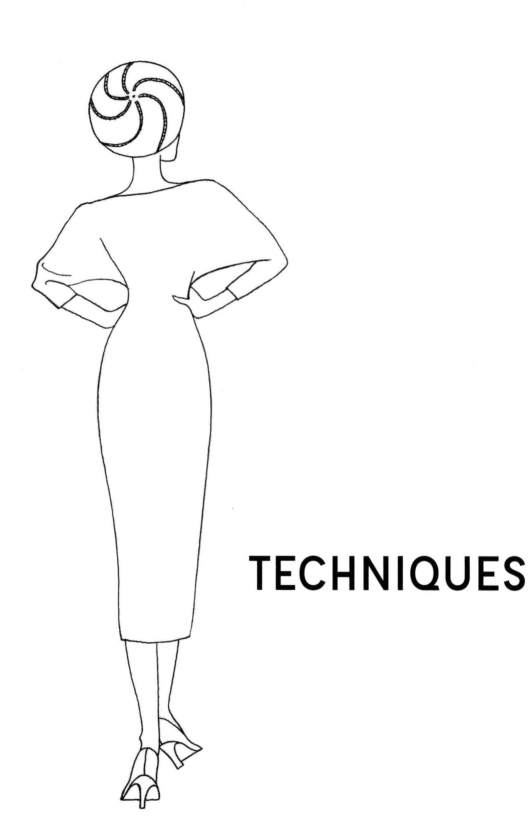

TECHNIQUES

Getting Started

The list of materials at the beginning of each pattern will show you everything you will need to gather together before starting the project.

HOOKS

Crochet hook sizes vary widely, from tiny hooks that produce a very fine stitch when used with threads, to oversized hooks for working with several strands of yarn at one time to create a bulky fabric. Using a larger or smaller hook will change the look of the fabric; it will also affect the tension and the amount of yarn required. The projects in this book use hooks ranging in size from 3.25mm (UK10:USD/3) to 10mm (UK 000:USN–P/15).

NEEDLES

A blunt-ended yarn needle is used to sew the projects together. The large eye makes it easy to thread the needle and the rounded end will prevent any snagging.

SUBSTITUTING YARNS

When substituting yarns, it is important to calculate the number of balls required by the number of yards or metres per ball, rather than the weight of the yarn, because this varies according to the fibre. Tension is also important. Always work a tension swatch in the yarn you wish to use before starting a project.

READING INSTRUCTIONS

The hat patterns are written in three sizes. The smallest size is given first; where the larger instructions differ, the adjustments are given inside the square brackets []. If O appears in the instructions, then no stitches, rounds or rows are to be worked for this size. Where there is no bracket after the stitches, rounds or rows given, the instructions refer to all sizes.

READING CHARTS

Each symbol on a chart represents a stitch; each round or row represents one round or row of crochet.

For rounds of crochet, read the chart anti-clockwise, starting at the centre and working out to the last round on the chart.

For rows of crochet, the chart should be read back and forth, following the number at the beginning of each row.

The charts are shown in alternate rounds or rows of blue and black. The last round or row from a previous chart is shown in grey.

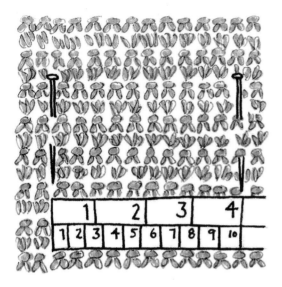

STITCHES

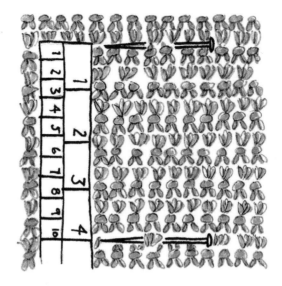

ROWS

TENSION

It is vital to check your tension before starting a project, as this will affect the size and look of the hat, as well as the amount of yarn you will use. The tension is the number of rows and stitches per square inch or centimetre of crocheted fabric.

Using the same size hook and type of stitch as stated in the pattern, work a sample of around 5in (12.5cm) square and then smooth it out on a flat surface.

Stitches

Place a ruler horizontally across the work and mark 4in (10cm) with pins. Count the number of stitches between the pins, including half stitches. This will give you the tension of stitches.

Rows

Measure the tension of rows by placing a ruler vertically over the work and mark 4in (10cm) with pins. Count the number of rows between the pins.

If the number of stitches and rows is greater than those stated in the pattern, your tension is tighter and you should use a larger hook. If the number of stitches and rows is smaller than those stated in the pattern, your tension is looser, so you should use a smaller hook.

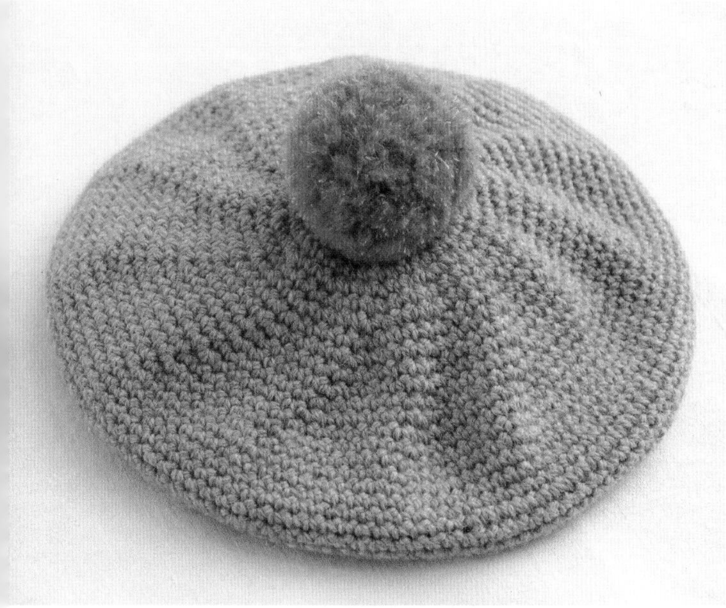

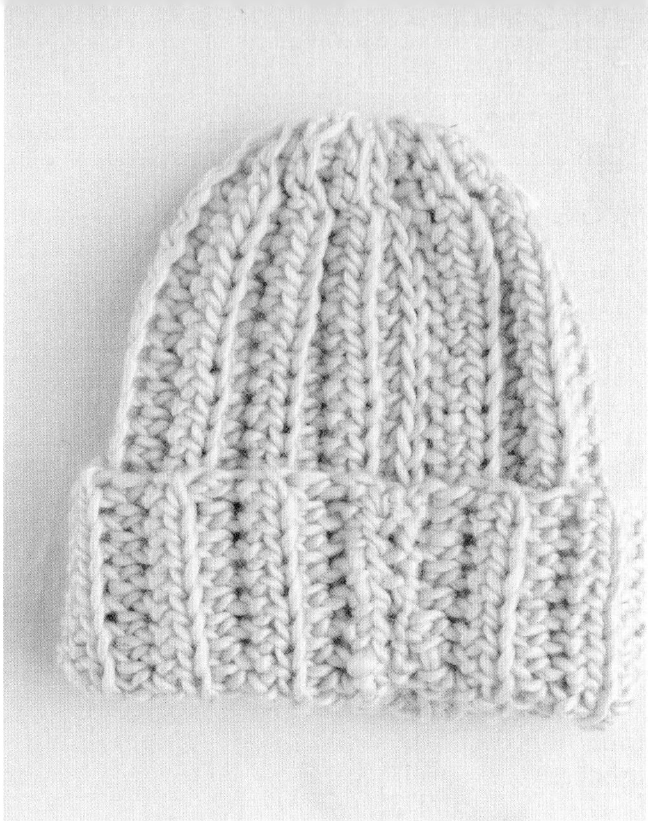

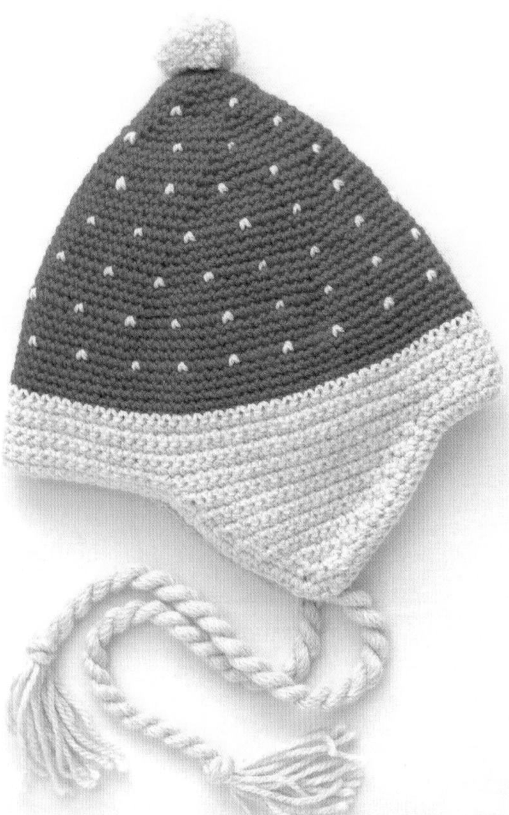

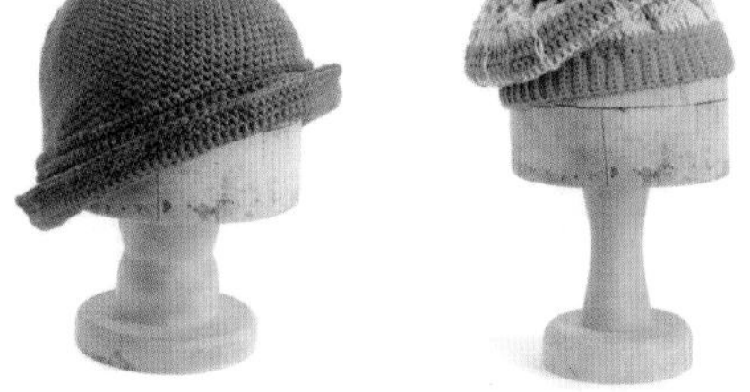

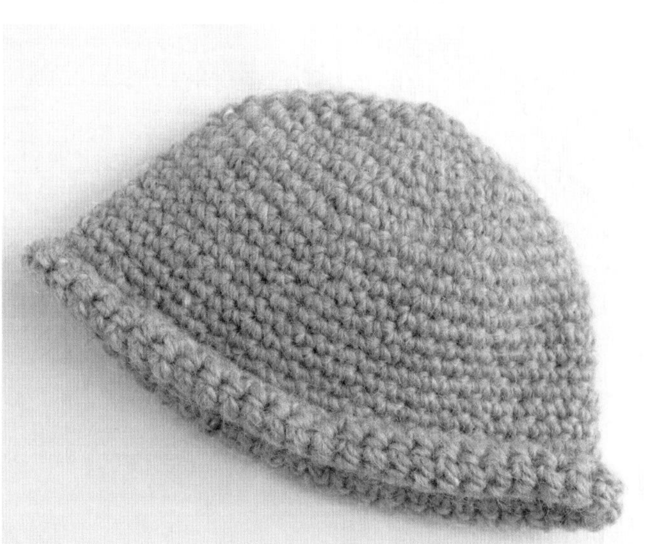

Crochet Stitches

Here you will find the basic information on how to hold the hook and yarn, crocheting the various stitches and joining in a new colour.

SLIP KNOT

Take the end of the yarn and form it into a loop. Holding it in place between thumb and forefinger, insert the hook through the loop, catch the long end that is attached to the ball, and draw it back through. Keeping the yarn looped on the hook, pull through until the loop closes around the hook, ensuring it is not tight. Pulling on the short end of yarn will loosen the knot, while pulling on the long end will tighten it.

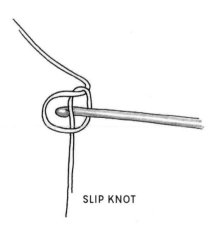

SLIP KNOT

HOLDING THE WORK
Hook

Hold the hook as you would a pencil, bringing your middle finger forward to rest near the tip of the hook. This will help control the movement of the hook, while the fingers of your other hand will regulate the tension of the yarn. The hook should face you, pointing slightly downwards. The motion of the hook and yarn should be free and even, not tight. This will come with practice.

Yarn

To hold your work and control the tension, pass the yarn over the first two fingers of your left hand (right if you are left-handed), under the third finger and around the little finger, and let the yarn fall loosely to the ball. As you work, take the stitch you made between the thumb and forefinger of the same hand.

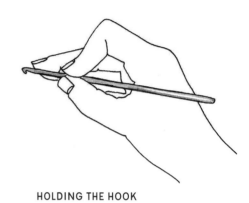

HOLDING THE HOOK

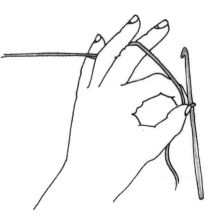

HOLDING THE YARN

MAGIC LOOP

Many of the crocheted pieces start with an adjustable loop of yarn. To make the loop, wind the yarn around a finger, insert the hook, catch the yarn and draw back through the loop. After a couple of rounds have been crocheted, covering the loop of yarn, the short end of yarn is pulled tight to close the centre. An alternative method is to make four chain stitches and then slip stitch to the first chain to form a ring. However, this technique does leave a hole in the middle.

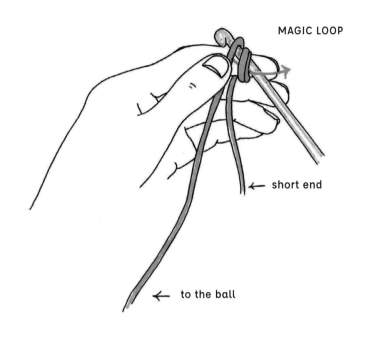

MAGIC LOOP

← short end

← to the ball

CHAIN (ch)

1

2

CHAIN (ch)

1 Pass the hook under and over the yarn that is held taut between the first and second fingers. This is called 'yarn round hook' (yrh). Draw the yarn through the loop on the hook. This makes one chain (ch).

2 Repeat step 1, keeping the thumb and forefinger of the left hand close to the hook, until you have as many chain stitches as required.

SLIP STITCH (sl st)

Make a practice chain of 10. Insert hook into first stitch (st), yrh, draw through both loops on hook. This forms 1 slip stitch (sl st).
Continue to end. This will give you 10 slip stitches (10 sts).

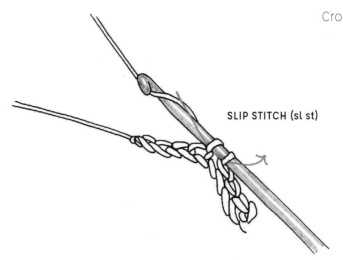

SLIP STITCH (sl st)

DOUBLE CROCHET (dc)

Make a practice chain of 17. Skip the first ch.

1 Insert hook from front into the next stitch, yrh and draw back through the stitch (2 loops on hook).

2 Yrh and draw through 2 loops (1 loop on hook). This makes one double crochet (dc).

Repeat steps 1 and 2 to the end of the row. On the foundation chain of 17 sts, you should have 16 double crochet sts (16 sts).

Next row

Turn the work so the reverse side faces you. Make 1 ch. This is the turning chain, which helps keep a neat edge and does not count as a stitch. Rep steps 1 and 2 to the end of the row. Continue until the desired number of rows is complete. Fasten off.

FASTENING OFF

When you have finished, fasten off by cutting the yarn around 4³⁄₄in (12cm) from the work. Draw the loose end through the remaining loop, pulling it tightly.

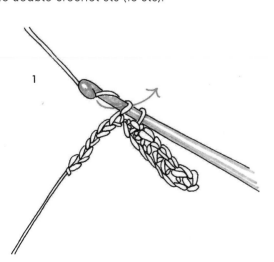

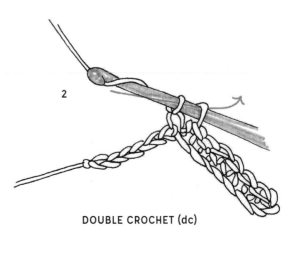

DOUBLE CROCHET (dc)

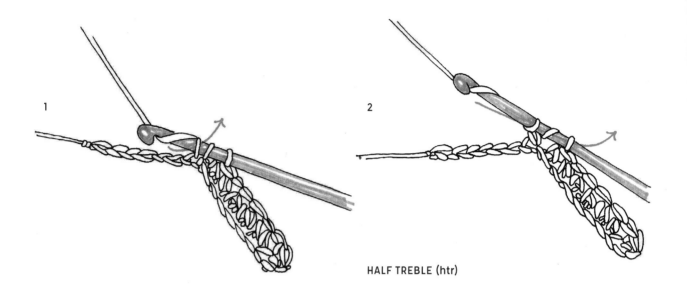

HALF TREBLE (htr)

HALF TREBLE (htr)

Make a practice chain of 17. Skip the first 2 ch (these count as the first half treble stitch).

1 Yrh, insert hook into the next stitch, yrh and draw back through stitch (3 loops on hook).

2 Yrh, draw through all 3 loops (1 loop on hook).
This forms 1 half treble (htr).

Repeat steps 1 and 2 to the end of the row. On the foundation chain of 17 sts, you should have 16 half trebles (16 sts), including the 2 ch at the beginning of the row, which is counted as the first stitch.

Next row

Turn the work so the reverse side faces you. Make 2 ch to count as the first half treble. Skip the first stitch of the previous row. Repeat steps 1 and 2 for the next 14 htr of the last row, work 1 htr in the second of the 2 ch at the end of the row. Continue until the desired number of rows is complete. Fasten off.

TREBLE (tr)

Make a practice chain of 18. Skip the first 3 ch stitches (these count as the first tr).

1 Yrh, insert hook into the next stitch, yarn round hook and draw back through the stitch (3 loops on hook).

2 Yrh, draw through 2 loops (2 loops on hook).

3 Yrh, draw through 2 loops (1 loop on hook). This forms 1 treble (tr).

Repeat steps 1–3 to end of row.

On the foundation chain of 18 sts you should have 16 trebles (16 sts), including the 3 ch at the beginning of the row, which is counted as the first stitch.

Next row

Turn the work so the reverse side faces you. Make 3 ch to count as the first treble. Skip the first stitch of the previous row. Repeat steps 1–3 to the end of the row, working 1 tr into the third of the 3 ch at the beginning of the last row. Continue until the desired number of rows is complete. Fasten off.

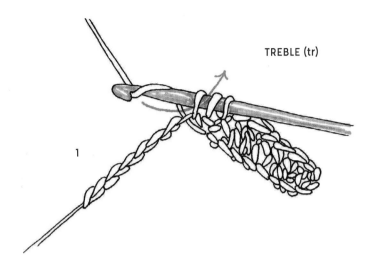

TREBLE (tr)

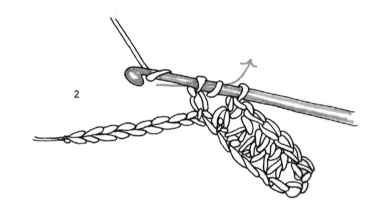

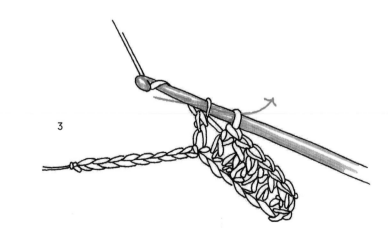

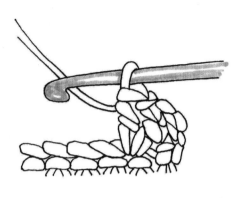

INCREASE

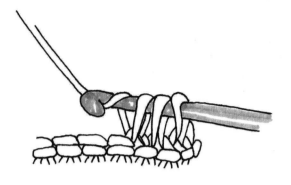

DECREASE

INCREASING

To increase one double crochet (dc2inc), work two stitches into one stitch of the previous row.

DECREASING

To decrease one double crochet (dc2tog), insert the hook into the next st, yrh and draw back through the stitch (2 loops on hook); insert the hook into the following st, yrh and draw back through the st (3 loops on hook), yrh and draw through all three loops on the hook.

WORKING INTO THE BACK OR FRONT LOOP ONLY

The front loop of a stitch is the one closer to you and the back loop is the stitch further away. Generally, the hook is inserted into both loops of a stitch, but when only one loop is crocheted into, the horizontal bar of the remaining loop is left on the surface of the fabric. This method is used in a number of the projects, such as the peak of the cap and the ribbed hat pattern on pages 18 and 74.

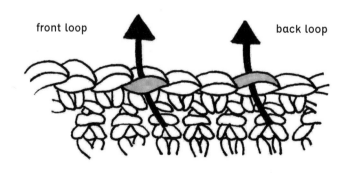

front loop   back loop

WORKING INTO THE BACK OR FRONT LOOP ONLY

WORKING WITH MULTIPLE COLOURS

Joining a new colour

When joining in a new colour at the beginning of a round or middle of a row, work the last step of the stitch in the new colour. Catch the yarn in the new colour and draw through the loops on the hook to complete the stitch.

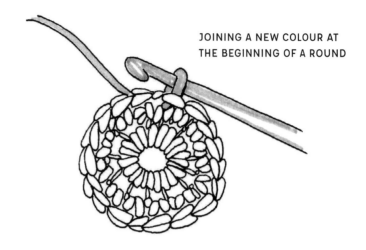

JOINING A NEW COLOUR AT
THE BEGINNING OF A ROUND

Carrying unused yarn across the work

When the colour that is not in use is to be carried across the wrong side of the work, it can be hidden along the line of stitches being made by working over the unused strand every few stitches with the new colour. When both sides of the work will be visible, the unused strand is worked over on every stitch, keeping the crocheted fabric neat on both sides. Lay the strand not being used on top of the previous row of stitches and crochet over it in the new colour, covering the unused colour. This method is used for the fairisle hat on page 89.

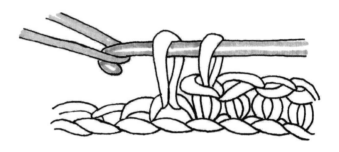

JOINING A NEW COLOUR IN
THE MIDDLE OF A ROW

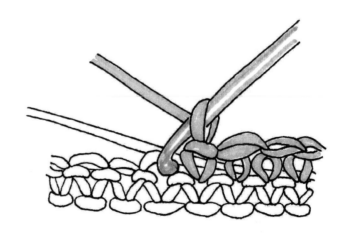

CARRYING UNUSED YARN
ACROSS THE WORK

Seams

When sewing up the seams, use safety pins or glass-headed dressmaker's pins to hold the pieces together. Here are a couple of seams that can be used to finish off the crocheted hats.

RIGHT-SIDE SEAM

This method is completed on the right side of the piece and produces a strong, flat and invisible seam.

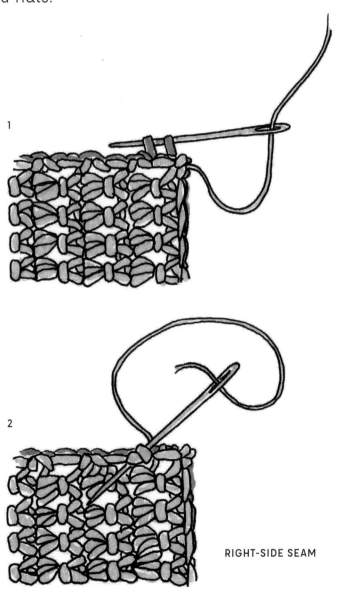

1 With wrong sides of the work together, attach the yarn to one piece of the work to be joined, insert the needle in from the back to the front of the other piece of the work, catching one loop of the edge stitch. Then insert the needle a little further along the same piece of the work, from the front to the back and draw up the yarn tightly.

2 Insert the needle into the first piece of the work from the front to the back, catching one loop of the edge stitch as before. Then insert the needle a little further along the same edge from the back to the front of the work and draw up the yarn tightly.

Continue in this way to the end.

RIGHT-SIDE SEAM

BACK STITCH

This method is carried out on the wrong side of the work. Work close to the edges of the pieces for a neat finish.

Begin by working a couple of stitches over each other to secure the seam. Bring the needle through to the front of the work one stitch ahead of the last stitch made. Then insert the needle back through the work at the end of the last stitch.

Repeat to complete the seam, making sure your stitches are neat.

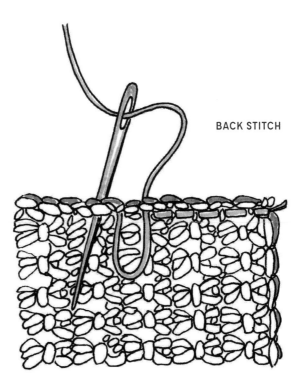

BACK STITCH

ABBREVIATIONS

ch	chain
cm	centimetre(s)
dc	double crochet
dc2inc	work 2 double crochet stitches into the next stitch to increase
dc2tog	work 2 double crochet stitches together to decrease
dec	decrease
htr	half treble
in	inches
inc	increase
m	metre(s)
mm	millimetre(s)
rep	repeat
RS	right side
sl st	slip stitch
sp	space
st(s)	stitch(es)
tog	together
tr	treble
WS	wrong side
yd	yards
yrh	yarn round hook

UK/US CROCHET TERMS

UK	US
Double crochet	Single crochet
Half treble	Half double crochet
Treble	Double crochet

Note: This book uses UK crochet terms

CONVERSIONS

STEEL CROCHET HOOKS

UK	Metric	US
6	0.60mm	14
5½	–	13
5	0.75mm	12
4½	–	11
4	1.00mm	10
3½	–	9
3	1.25mm	8
2½	1.50mm	7
2	1.75mm	6
1½	–	5

STANDARD CROCHET HOOKS

UK	Metric	US
14	2mm	–
13	2.25mm	B/1
12	2.5mm	–
–	2.75mm	C/2
11	3mm	–
10	3.25mm	D/3
9	3.5mm	E/4
–	3.75mm	F/5
8	4mm	G/6
7	4.5mm	7
6	5mm	H/8
5	5.5mm	I/9
4	6mm	J/10
3	6.5mm	K/10.5
2	7mm	–
0	8mm	L/11
00	9mm	M–N/13
000	10mm	N–P/15

RESOURCES

YARN

Canada
Cascade Yarns
www.cascadeyarns.com

Germany
Rico Design
www.rico-design.de

Iceland
Álafoss
www.alafoss.is

Norway
Drops Design
www.garnstudio.com

The Netherlands
Scheepjes
www.scheepjes.com

UK
Deramores
www.deramores.com

King Cole Ltd
www.kingcole.co.uk

LoveCrafts Ltd
www.lovecrafts.com

Patons
www.knitpatons.com

The Stitchery
www.the-stitchery.co.uk

Wool Warehouse
www.woolwarehouse.co.uk

USA
Purl Soho
www.purlsoho.com

CROCHET HOOKS

UK
LoveCrafts Ltd
(see under Yarn)

The Stitchery
(see under Yarn)

Wool Warehouse
(see under Yarn)

USA
Purl Soho
(see under Yarn)

BUCKLES

UK
Vintage Button Emporium
www.vintagebuttonemporium.com

The Swagman's Daughter
www.theswagmansdaughter.com

ACKNOWLEDGEMENTS

Thank you to Jonathan Bailey for giving me
the opportunity to write *Simple Crocheted Hats*.
Thank you Sara Harper, Rebecca Mothersole,
Emma Foster and to all at GMC. Neal Grundy,
Lindsey Poole and Julia L at MOT Models.
I dedicate this book to my family: Damian,
Miriam, Dilys, Flynn, Honey, Dolly, Leo and
Winter, who I have loved making hats for and
who kindly modelled these hats as I tweaked
and adjusted the patterns. I would particularly
like to thank four-year-old Winter; she stood
very patiently while I measured her head and
tried various hats on her almost every day
throughout the making of this book!

Index

First published 2019 by
Guild of Master Craftsman Publications Ltd Castle Place,
166 High Street, Lewes, East Sussex, BN7 1XU, UK

Text © Vanessa Mooncie, 2019

Copyright in the Work © GMC Publications Ltd, 2019

ISBN 978 1 78494 540 4

All rights reserved.

The right of Vanessa Mooncie to be identified as the author
of this work has been asserted in accordance with the
Copyright, Designs and Patents Act 1988, sections 77 and
78. No part of this publication may be reproduced, stored
in a retrieval system or transmitted in any form or by any
means without the prior permission of the publisher and
copyright owner.

This book is sold subject to the condition that all designs
are copyright and are not for commercial reproduction
without the permission of the designer and copyright
owner. While every effort has been made to obtain
permission from the copyright holders for all material used
in this book, the publishers will be pleased to hear from
anyone who has not been appropriately acknowledged and
to make the correction in future reprints.

The publishers and author can accept no legal responsibility
for any consequences arising from the application of
information, advice or instructions given in this publication.
A catalogue record for this book is available from the
British Library.

Publisher Jonathan Bailey
Production Manager Jim Bulley
Senior Project Editor Sara Harper
Editor Nicola Hodgson
Managing Art Editor Gilda Pacitti
Art Editor Rebecca Mothersole
Photographers Neal Grundy and Rebecca Mothersole
Make-up Lindsey Poole
Model Julia L, MOT Models
Illustrations Vanessa Mooncie

Colour origination by GMC Reprographics
Printed and bound in Turkey

To order a book, or to request a catalogue, contact:
GMC Publications Ltd, Castle Place, 166 High Street, Lewes,
East Sussex, BN7 1XU, UK
Tel : +44(0)1273 488005
www.gmcbooks.com